Living with the Devil

Living with the Devil

HE WAS SO CRUEL,
BUT I LOVED HIM SO MUCH.
THIS IS THE TRUE STORY OF
HOW I REBUILT MY LIFE

AMY NORMAN

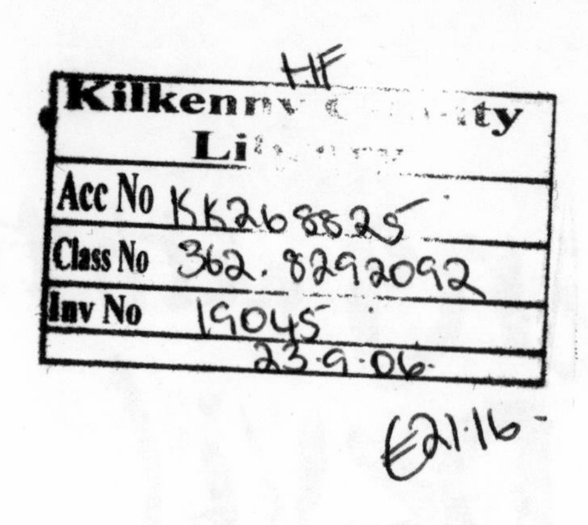

Published by John Blake Publishing Ltd,
3, Bramber Court, 2 Bramber Road,
London W14 9PB, England

www.blake.co.uk

First published in Great Britain in 2006 by John Blake Publishing Ltd.

First published by Bantam in 2005

ISBN 1 84454 211 4

British Library Cataloguing-in-Publication Data:

A catalogue record for this book is available from the British Library.

Design by www.envydesign.co.uk

Printed and bound in Great Britain by William Clowes Ltd, Beccles, Suffolk

1 3 5 7 9 10 8 6 4 2

Papers used by John Blake Publishing are natural, recyclable products made from wood grown in sustainable forests. The manufacturing processes conform to the environmental regulations of the country of origin.

To Mum and Dad
for always being there.

And to my amazing children
for giving me the strength to fight
and the determination to succeed.

Pseudonyms have been used and other details altered throughout to protect the identity of people and organisations mentioned in this book.

Prologue

'Battle not with monsters,
Lest ye become a monster.
And if you gaze into the abyss,
The abyss gazes into you.'

– FRIEDRICH NIETZSCHE

In the devil's world chaos rules, Satan is an inspiration and love knows no existence. Light is extinguished like a flickering candle on the back of a cool breeze, and the warmth of life disappears, to be replaced by cold terror and dark shadows hovering like vultures, silently waiting, invading your dreams, your thoughts, your soul. Destroying your very being, everything you are and everything you thought you could be.

My world changed forever the day the devil chose me. Embracing me tightly, seductively, sucking the life from me, making me his own. Ensnaring me in a world which was unfamiliar, a world where people got what they wanted, no matter the means or the consequence. This was his world.

A world where drugs, alcohol, violence and crime are normal pastimes and often lead to profitable and acceptable ways of living. If you can't get it yourself, then just take it from someone else. It doesn't matter who you step on, as long as nobody steps on you. Life is fast, cruel and dangerous.

The devil's hold is hypnotic, mesmerising. Don't be fooled, there is no escape, he will make you feel that you are the only one for him, the only one who can satisfy him. That he is the only one who can satisfy you.

The devil has many faces and you are going to meet them all. I have been up close and personal, I have looked in his eyes and I have seen my life explode in them like a shooting star in a black sky. I have seen his chaos and tasted his acid hatred. I have felt the tremendous force of his existence and the power of his reign.

In order to survive I needed to learn the rules of the game. And I did; I learnt to play his twisted games better than he did. I mastered his deceitful, cunning ways. I learnt to seek protection from the same people I feared and I learnt that things are not always as they seem.

I am not sure how much exists of the person I once was, but in her place stands a powerful, resilient woman who is no longer scared of the shadows.

Heaven, I have not yet seen. Hell, I have lived.

PART 1

Black and Blue

Chapter 1

I stopped to take in the view, my legs burning from the climb. It was beautiful up here, I remembered the sense of peace I used to feel and let its welcome relief wash over me, flooding every tiny pore.

I sat at the edge of the cliff, my feet dangling towards the tree-filled valley below. The branches of the tallest eucalypts reached for me, as if to shroud me in their embrace should I fall. This was my mountain; it knew my deepest secrets, my darkest thoughts. It knew my fears, my hopes and my dreams. It knew how to soothe me in times of despair, and I had been gone too long.

I felt its welcome in the faintest breath of a breeze gently caressing my cheeks, in the rays of light gleaming through the green canopy above. I closed my eyes and breathed as deeply as I could, filling my lungs with its raw, fresh beauty.

I tilted my head toward the clear blue sky, squinting

through the bright streaks of golden sunlight. As a child I had imagined these rays were angels shining their light upon me, protecting me. Enveloping me in their wisdom, strength and courage. I wished they would come back. I squinted my eyes some more and tried to conjure up the images so easily seen back then. Though, as with everything sent to comfort me as a child, my angels were nowhere to be found.

I shifted my attention back to the hills stretched out before me, gazing over the abundance of trees covering the valley floor, their massive crowns protecting all that lives beneath them. I concentrated on the bright colours of the rosellas flitting between branches, listening intently to their chatter.

No matter how long I was gone, this mountain never changed. No matter how many changes took place in my world, no matter how many tears I cried or how many mistakes I made, the mountain remained the same.

I remembered standing in this very spot almost eleven years ago, trying to learn by heart every inch. Every tree, every rock, everything my eyes could see, everything my fingers could touch, wanting to burn the images into my mind, never to be forgotten. That day no golden rays of light shone through the trees, there were no thoughts of angels, there was no happiness and hope seemed very far away.

I wanted to throw myself off that cliff. The only thing stopping me was the child I carried, its restlessness awakening me from my thoughts of self-harm, dread and fear. What kind of life was I bringing this baby into? My hands automatically encircled my growing belly, lovingly, protectively.

As fresh tears fell from my already swollen eyes I felt the baby kick once more, as if she too could feel my sadness. Confusing thoughts of the past few months entered my already addled mind. This wasn't how I had imagined things to be.

A crow flew swiftly by me, circling the valley, echoing my cries in his own sad sound. I touched my head, which had begun to ache again and flinched at the pain, quickly pulling my hand away.

Why did he hit me? What did I do? These questions raced continuously through my mind, but always remained unanswered. I wasn't sure whether it was because there wasn't an answer. Or whether I was just too stupid to see it.

As the last of the dull orange sun descended behind the hills I knew I had to go, but I was reluctant to leave my private oasis. I didn't want to go back down there. It was like the land of the living dead, and I did not want to become one of them. I was tired, alone and pregnant. Dean didn't care. He had changed, and seemed to find more pleasure in hurting me than in loving me.

Lately the only times he showed that familiar, tender

side was when he apologised for the pain he inflicted. Which he always did, and I always forgave him. I think deep down I knew even then that I shouldn't, but my baby needed a father and I knew I couldn't do it alone. I was eighteen and shit-scared, I actually had visions of dying in childbirth. The nightmares terrified me. Sometimes in my imaginings the child which had burst forth from my body closely resembled the grotesque shape of the elephant man. I was completely freaked out, and I hated pain.

I had been chased around a doctor's surgery when I was ten years old because I didn't want a needle. My father, who is not a small man by any stretch of the imagination, had to sit on me just so the nice doctor could torture me. If there is a way of avoiding pain I will find it. I had drilled the doctors at the hospital more times than I could count about the various drugs available to me during labour, knowing I would welcome each and every one with open arms.

I walked up the steps to the front door, hearing the racket of the unsavoury neighbourhood we called home. Children crying, sirens wailing, dogs barking, people yelling – it was a never-ending sequence of unwelcome and at times alarming sounds.

This is the place where scum thrives, and hope dies. The world somehow lacks colour here, as though the artist was suddenly left with only dull brown and grey hues on his normally bright palette. A morbid playground where the devil rules his followers, where no-one is safe from him or from what he has to offer. It is a drug addict's wonderland, an alcoholic's heaven and a criminal's safe haven. The worst things you could possibly imagine are sure to exist here, a place where not only children check in cupboards and under beds for the bogeyman.

I let myself into the dark house and was relieved to find Dean was not there. I turned on the kitchen light and found a note on the table. Two words were written on the torn paper in large red letters:

FUCK YOU

Over the next few weeks everything was fine, it was as though the horror of the past months had not occurred. As though Dean had never hurt me. Or told me I was stupid and ugly. It was as though nothing had happened at all. Maybe Dean was right; maybe that reality had truly existed only in my head. He confidently sat me down and explained that my hormones were going crazy. Apparently pregnancy was screwing with my mind.

'It happens to some women,' he said. He was quite serious and I believed him. I always believed him. He could have been running around in circles telling me the sky was falling in and I would have believed him.

What did I know? I was young, silly and naive. Dean was four years older than me. We'd met at a party and I'd thought he was the best-looking man I had ever seen,

I had been flattered that he had paid me so much attention. Our relationship developed very quickly. After the night of the party we became virtually inseparable. He had made me feel special. His huge frame towered over me and I felt safe wrapped in his arms. He would look down at me with his piercing blue eyes and promise to always protect me. I believed nothing could ever hurt me with Dean by my side. I didn't know then that less than twelve months later, it was Dean I would begin to fear. He would no longer make me feel safe or special.

For now, though, the fear had dissipated and we were both content to prepare for our new arrival. In the beginning stages of the pregnancy Dean had not attended the regular prenatal appointments with me. He didn't seem to want to concern himself with the development of his son or daughter.

I, on the other hand, was enthralled with the changes occurring in my body. There were new wonders to behold daily. The most fascinating of these were my newfound breasts. They had grown like ripening melons and I was concerned they might never stop.

There were other 'wonders', however, that I would have gladly done without. For instance the constant nausea and exhaustion. Swollen feet and aching legs, not to mention the astounding realisation that not being able to see your own feet can make walking down stairs a difficult and, I worried, potentially fatal task. It was the simple things you took for granted, like sleeping on your stomach. How

I missed that! Life is certainly made interesting the day you realise you have grown too large to heave your enormous bulk out of the couch.

This hadn't been a planned pregnancy, neither of us had expected it, but we had decided to go ahead and do the best we could. If things had gone bad at that point I think my decision would have been entirely different.

But things hadn't changed until it was too late to go back. Too late to undo all that had been done. Too late to see how the events taking place would dramatically alter the path my life was to take.

'Jesus Christ,' Dean was staring at me with a look on his face that I had never seen before. Was it shock, or disgust? I couldn't tell. It probably matched the startled look on my own face as a huge gush of liquid exploded from between my legs, splashing over the kitchen floor.

'Oh my God. Quick, get me something.' I didn't know exactly what I wanted him to get, I could only feel panic begin to surface. My waters had broken, God help me, it was starting.

I felt a sudden surge of red heat rush through my body. I was sure I was going to pass out any minute. Dean had disappeared somewhere and I was left standing in a puddle of my own bodily fluids with my hands in a sink full of soapy dishwater.

Dean reappeared with the bag I had meticulously

packed months ago, in anticipation of this moment. I couldn't move, I was planted to the spot, my feet moulding with the grey linoleum floor covering. My mind was a swirling mass of blank matter unable to decide what to do next.

So my body took over: it made no difference whether my brain agreed or not. The brain was now obsolete. Co-operation was not needed between the two to handle this job.

A sharp pain shot through my abdomen, causing me to double over. It lasted only a second but I wasn't sure I really wanted to continue with this. It was only the beginning – the first real pain, apart from the niggling sensations that had been bothering me all day.

Dean put the bag by the front door and helped me to the bathroom to get changed. There was no way I was walking into the hospital looking like I had a bladder control problem. It would have been quite obvious to anyone that I was having a baby, but I didn't want to lose my dignity until I really had to, which was sure to happen before this was over.

Parts of the next 25 hours remain a blur; the gas made me sick, the pain was unbearable and I begged for the drugs they had promised me. Dean wanted the bed because he was tired – I wanted to castrate him and when the pethidine finally arrived I was grateful. Only until the next contraction, however – the pain was still as bad as it had been, the liars.

'Just get me a knife,' I yelled. I was positive that cutting myself open would tickle compared to this. And when the time came to push, I thought I would split in two.

'You did it,' whispered Dean. As our daughter slid from my body, his smile stretched from ear to ear.

Yep, I did, didn't I? The baby was placed on my now empty belly, all red and slimy, her small lungs working hard as her cries filled the room.

I couldn't speak, all I could do was look at her. This tiny person had lived inside me. She was a part of me.

The pain was quickly forgotten. In its place was a feeling of love so powerful it consumed me, warmed me, made me feel so light I imagined I would lift off the bed and float away like a soft cloud. I had never felt so alive. I looked up at Dean. Amazement covered his handsome face. Did he feel the same? Did he feel this alive too, as though every nerve in his body had been electrified? I wondered if he felt as invincible as I did at that moment. I didn't feel the exhaustion I should have felt. I felt like I could run a marathon.

Little Kate weighed in at 7 lb 1 oz and arrived home five days later. She was proudly introduced to everyone we knew. Dean behaved like the doting father one would expect and his daughter was the image of him. She had his dark hair and complexion – there seemed few, if any of my fair features. Not that I cared who she looked like, she was healthy and she was beautiful. Nothing like the elephant baby I had dreamed of.

I was happy.

I would sit for hours and watch as Dean slept with Kate dreaming sweetly on his chest. I loved to see her nestled within his great arms. Seeing this made me feel more love for him than I had ever felt. What was it about a man and his baby? It made my heart race; there is something uniquely sexy about it.

Within a few weeks our peaceful, sleepy bundle of joy turned into a screaming bundle of ear-piercing noise that lasted day and night. She no longer slept, only cried, which meant I no longer slept and often, through utter exhaustion, joined her in chorus.

The doting father swiftly departed, leaving in his place the stranger I had seen before and hoped would not meet again.

'What kind of fuckin' mother are you? You can't even shut your own kid up,' he yelled at me before slamming the door so hard the wall shook.

I didn't know what kind of mother I was; I had never done this before. It would have been much easier if babies came with instructions. I felt useless enough without Dean putting me down. I was sleep-deprived, moving mostly on automatic pilot, and his constant barrage of insults put me on edge. Kate had been in our lives for only eight weeks; it felt like a lifetime.

One morning Dean stormed into the bedroom. I was pacing the floor holding Kate, singing softly to her, praying she would fall asleep and give me a reprieve. Dean ripped her from me, forcefully put her in her cot, grabbed my arm tightly and pulled me out of the room, slamming the door behind him.

'No, no, Dean don't, I have to go back in there,' I begged, his hold still firm on my arm.

'No you won't, you'll leave the little bitch,' he spat at me. As the shrieking escalated behind the door my panic grew. What if something happened? What if she choked? What if she stopped breathing? These thoughts whizzed through my head at a hundred miles an hour. I couldn't leave my baby in there alone, she needed me.

'Let me go, Dean,' I said as forcefully as I could. He tightened his grip and moved closer to me; I could feel his breath in my ear.

'No,' was all he said.

Dean had been spending a lot of time with his friends. If he wasn't out with them, they were at our place. They were a rowdy bunch of blokes when they got together and it made it hard with a baby in the house. I didn't really mind though, I liked his friends; we used to have a lot of fun.

I was sitting at the kitchen table enjoying the peace and quiet with a cup of tea and the newspaper when they arrived.

'You guys had better keep it down,' I said as they piled into the tiny room.

'Yeah. Well, don't you want any of this?' Beck was

grinning at me cheekily, holding a sandwich bag filled with the familiar tight green buds of marijuana. He was moving the bag in front of my face as if trying to hypnotise me.

Beck was my favourite of all the guys. He looked like a big bear and was like the brother I never had. I was looking at the bag still dangling before my eyes. I hadn't been stoned for ages and considered it a welcome distraction.

It was these guys who had really taught me to smoke. They introduced me to joints, bucket bongs and party cones. They showed me how to improvise; I learnt how to make bongs out of Coke cans, and babies' bottles. If a proper cone wasn't available, a thimble with a hole in the bottom or one modelled from aluminium foil would suffice.

We were crowded around the small table, sweet smoke filling the air. Dean handed me the ceramic bong that had been shaped into a skull and I slowly lit the cone, pulling the hot smoke into my lungs. The guys were amazed that I could pull such a big cone in one hit. They always joked about having to pack what they called a budgie cone for a girl.

Not this girl though, I was determined to keep up with them. I learnt very quickly that if you could do things as well as them, if not better, they would respect you.

I had found boys to be a lot more fun than girls to hang out with. I didn't like giggling and I didn't like gossip. Boys were so much more exciting; they tested the limits and disregarded boundaries.

Not long after I met Dean they taught me to drive fast

cars, and I had soon mastered the art of the perfect burnout. This had been my first taste, my first lesson in gaining acceptance. Every Saturday night there were burnout contests in empty parking lots. Hoons from all over would show up in loud, fancy cars. Some had exhaust pipes so big they sounded like rockets launching into space.

When I was put behind the wheel of Beck's powerful V8 Commodore the looks on the faces of the tattoo-covered gaolbirds who frequented these events was priceless. They must have thought he was mad. It was a beautiful car, white with a huge silver bug-catcher fitted to the bonnet. I loved the feel of its power, the squeal of the tyres, the smell of the burning rubber, the rumble of the engine.

Here I was, this little girl who was only just old enough to drive, and I was being admired for destroying car tyres. It seems ridiculous to me now, but I had never had so much fun in my life.

From that day on, the guys invaded my home on a regular basis and smoko became a daily event. Kate would lie in her bouncer gurgling quietly to herself as the dark grey skull pipe was passed around the room. I looked forward to these times. It blurred my reality and somehow made things look a little more colourful.

Before long I was the one sent to acquire the stuff. I became known to every dealer in the area. I often spent hours doing the rounds; demand was high and the product wasn't always available from the same person. This sticky, strong-smelling plant was more precious than gold and quickly became my best friend. It relieved stress, helped me sleep, and made me hungry. When I was overcome with the munchies anything and everything looked good enough to eat.

My numerous trips to various drug dealers' homes were interesting and eye-opening experiences, to say the least. These minor lords came in all shapes and sizes: some were young, some were old and some were local policemen. These people could be your worst nightmare or your greatest saviour, depending on which individual you chose.

Our neighbourhood had at least eight drug havens. Here you could buy anything your heart desired. Many times the streets were jam-packed with cars, filled with people looking to quench their particular thirst. It was a volatile place to be when there was a shortage of what these addicts were after. These 'shops' were open 24 hours a day, so if you needed a fix in the middle of the night there was no need to hang out till morning. They were always there to take your money and, more often than not, to rip you off in the process. Most of the time you didn't care about the size of the deal, as long as you got one. The size only became a consideration once it was gone: how could it have disappeared so soon, surely you hadn't had that much, had you?

'C'mon, get the kid ready, she's going to Mum's, we're working tonight.'

'No, Dean. I told you I wasn't doing that any more.'

Dean was employed in the business of crime. This wasn't a new venture, just one I pretended to ignore most of the time. Early on I had been roped into being the lookout, my driving skills earning me the prestigious title of getaway driver. At first I had enjoyed the rush. It was small-time stuff really, break and enters – never homes, always businesses.

How did we justify it? Easy – businesses had insurance just for this purpose; we were actually doing them a favour. You can talk yourself into anything if you really want to, and as long as your conscience doesn't surface you're on easy street.

Drugs eased the conscience; to buy them you needed money and most of the time crime paid. I hadn't been involved in any of this for quite some time, and now that I had a baby I wanted nothing more to do with it. Dean was getting impatient.

'Jase is in the slammer and you're the only one there is. I'm not missin' out on this one, we've been casing the joint for ages.'

'But Dean, I don't want to.'

'I don't give a flyin' fuck what you want – just hurry up.'

An hour later Kate was at her grandmother's. This was the first time she had been away from me since she was born and I felt like I was missing a limb.

The four of us were sitting around the little wooden table familiarising ourselves with our individual roles. Dean, Beck and Shano were studying sketches they had made; it looked like they were preparing to break into a bank, not a tool factory. They had been there a few times before as customers so they could see what kind of alarm system had been installed. Alarms were easy to get around if you knew what you were doing.

Once the table was cleared Shano proceeded to get out the drug-taking paraphernalia. Pipes, marijuana, syringes, spoons and speed were carefully arranged. The boys took turns injecting themselves with the red liquid that would give them more courage than they normally had. I didn't do needles, so I soaked a piece of tissue, watching as it turned from white to red, and then swallowed it. That familiar metallic taste would keep me awake and make me walk on air. I always felt like I could fly on this stuff, it was like my feet didn't touch the ground. The speed, or goey as we referred to it, came in different forms depending on what was available at the time. Sometimes it was liquid, sometimes powder or sometimes crystals; we had used them all.

The car was parked in the garage. Dean had already replaced the numberplates with the stolen ones he had acquired for this purpose. We all dressed in dark clothing and the boys carried sports bags containing gloves, face masks, bolt cutters and crowbars. It was the strangest thing: the locals always wished us luck as we left and usually on our return came to see if we had anything that would be of use to them – for a price, of course. We had a really good barter system in place. If they wanted something from us and we wanted something from them, trading worked well and everyone was happy.

I drove carefully, making sure to stay under the speed limit, the drugs working to keep me alert, my vision sharp. Once we got to our destination I drove around the block a couple of times. We knew that security checked the factories in the area every four hours. We waited in the dark until the guards finished their next round, knowing we would have a good window of opportunity in which to work. We didn't need to hurry. The guys donned their masks and gloves.

'Make sure you're there in half an hour,' Dean said to me as they exited the car. I was to meet them at the rear entrance, parked as close to the gates as possible without being seen. I had a pillow and a blanket with me as my cover. If someone should come along, I would pretend to be asleep.

I drove around to the back of the building as we had planned, turning the lights and engine off and making my silent approach, slowly coasting to a standstill less than five metres from the tall iron gates.

I couldn't see anything that was happening inside and wished they would hurry up. Half an hour seemed like three – it was horrible sitting in that car. I was so hyped I couldn't sit still.

Before the half-hour had ticked over, the car boot was open and we were loading it up with power tools of all descriptions. Everything they had collected had been placed by the back door of the factory. Dean was passing them to Shano, who would then put them through the gates for myself and Beck to load. It was a very well worked production line and believe it or not we had actually practised this. We had done it over and over again, running from the house to the car with certain items, timing ourselves to see how much we could get in in the shortest time possible. We could have been world-class athletes in another life – our times were pretty amazing, and continued to get better and better. We could fill the car with thousands of dollars' worth of goods in no time at all.

It had been a good night and less than two days later each piece of stolen equipment had been sold. Dean would scour the papers for news of his handiwork. He behaved like an excited child at Christmas when the media took enough notice to report what he had done. For the first time I realised how sick this was.

Maybe he hadn't changed. Maybe motherhood had changed me. It was very confusing. Had he always been like this?

One thing that had changed, and very noticeably, was his controlling behaviour. He had begun to be extremely possessive and started giving me time limits whenever I left the house. The first time he did this was when I went out one morning to get some baby formula and nappies.

'You've got five minutes,' he growled at me. 'And you can leave her here.'

I handed Kate to him, grabbed the car keys and walked out the door, not thinking he was really serious. The mall was a ten-minute drive away, and that's only if you don't get held up at lights or stuck in traffic. Then there is the supermarket – they must think the longer they can keep you in there, the more money you will spend. They never have enough staff, and the ones they do have are so slow you wonder whether you should have brought a cut lunch.

I had been gone for 40 minutes. When I returned Dean was waiting for me just inside the door looking like he was ready to explode; his face was contorted in an angry expression.

'Hi. Where's Kate?' I asked as I surveyed the lounge room. I assumed she had cried while I was gone and this was the reason for his anger.

'Where have you been?' His voice was low and it shook slightly as if he were trying hard to maintain a calm front.

'I was at the shop.' I must have sounded confused, I had no idea what was going on. He knew where I'd been.

'Where else?' His voice had grown louder, his control fading.

'I didn't go anywhere else.'

'You fucking liar.' Before I knew what was happening I had hit the floor, my cheek stinging from the back-hander I had not seen coming. There was pain as my underwear was ripped roughly from my body. I felt disgusted when he lifted them to his face and breathed deeply, thoroughly, as if searching for something.

'I know you were out screwin' somebody. Who was it?'

'I don't know what you're talking about, Dean.' My voice was shaking now. I was still on the ground, not wanting to move, not knowing what he would do if I did. He suddenly forced me to my feet, his fingers digging into my arms. I heard Kate's faint cries coming from the bedroom as he dragged me to the couch.

'Dean, please stop. Please,' I begged, tears starting to roll down my face. He took no notice of my cries as he threw me on the soft cushions, forcing my legs apart.

'Dean, no!' I yelled, tears now cascading down my cheeks. I could taste the warm saltiness and my arms were pinned with crushing force above my head.

My eyes opened wide, stricken with terror as he painfully entered me, thrusting so hard I thought I might die.

❧

By the time Kate was six months old I rarely left the house unless I was ordered to go somewhere, which was usually to score drugs and only when Dean wanted them. Which, fortunately for me, was all the time. I could no longer survive reality. When I was high, I was numb, and numb was the only place to be.

Dean no longer called me by name. To him I was

a worthless piece of shit, which was exactly how he addressed me. As far as he was concerned I didn't deserve to breathe the same air as him. I never thought it was possible for people to be brainwashed. I thought such people weak. I now know better.

I had been told for so long that I was stupid and ugly, I started to believe it. I could no longer do anything right. I didn't wash the dishes right or wash his clothes right. I didn't hold the hose right to water the garden and if his dinner wasn't cooked to his liking it went flying across the room.

Every pension day he would leave with the money and not come back until it was gone. I would go for days at a time without food just so Kate would not starve. I began to lose weight rapidly and was constantly sick. I was so ashamed about everything that was happening that I could tell no-one.

I would sit for hours sobbing uncontrollably, Kate's head resting on my shoulder. She would wrap her chubby arms around me and kiss my cheek. Even before she was born this little girl knew how to comfort me.

I no longer saw my family; Dean didn't like me to in case they interfered. The last time I'd spoken to my mother on the phone he set the curtains alight just so I would hang up and put the fire out.

My parents had not been terribly happy about this relationship. But what could they do? I no longer lived at home so these decisions were mine to make.

My parents were kind and loving. They had provided my sisters and me with a safe, secure environment in which to grow up. We were spoilt and had everything we ever wanted. To me, my parents were perfect – I had never heard them say a bad word to each other, they never argued and they never fought. They sheltered us from all that was bad. I wasn't aware that evil existed in the world.

I had been given opportunities not offered to many kids. When I was nine I was invited to go overseas with a friend and her family. I travelled the world for eight weeks, missing my parents considerably. It was an opportunity I had been scared to take for I was worried that I would get lost and never find my way home. My parents talked me around, promising me everything would be fine. It was something I might never get to do again and they didn't want me to miss out on the trip of a lifetime.

When I was little I started ballet and dreamed of being a ballerina. I loved to dance. I felt comfortable on stage and I loved the attention. Between the ages of four and fifteen dancing was all I cared about.

I stopped dancing the day my teacher told me I was fat. That day all my dreams were shattered and everything I cared about changed. The one thing in my life I had been consistently passionate about no longer mattered. My fire had died and rebellion set in. Although this isn't the only thing that changed the course of my life, it is difficult to put my finger on the reason why this was a trigger. I have spent many hours contemplating this and don't think there was just one reason, but a multitude of them.

Maybe it was inconsistent parenting, lots of rules from my mother and none from my father. When Mum wasn't home my sisters and I could get away with anything. We learnt to be sneaky, keeping secrets from Mum and only asking Dad for permission to do certain things. I'm not sure he even heard us when we asked him, his eyes never left the television or the pages of a book he was reading. He would only grunt.

Maybe it was because we moved around constantly as I was growing up, resulting in a new school every couple of years and finding new ways to fit in.

Maybe it was just because I was spoilt and thought I was invincible. That nothing could ever go wrong. Bad things only happened to other people, not me. I started hanging out with the wrong crowd, the more exciting crowd. To be friends with them meant proving that I was worthy. So I started smoking cigarettes, smoking dope, drinking alcohol and staying out all night.

I no longer listened to my parents. I no longer listened to anyone. I did what I wanted, when I wanted. If trouble didn't find me, I went looking for trouble. At sixteen I left school, and home, and I thought I knew everything. A few months after I left home my family decided to move to the mountains. We had lived there for a couple of years when I was in primary school and it had been my favourite place as a child, spending my days in the bush climbing trees. My parents were moving over an hour away, leaving me behind. My choice, my mistake.

What I know now is that one wrong decision can affect your life forever. Bad things do happen.

Chapter 2

I didn't like people knowing things were not as they should be, and neither did Dean. To the outside world he was a tentative and loving partner. He was so convincing I didn't think anyone would believe me if I told them about the Dean I knew. The Dean I despised. Nobody else saw that side of him – he was like two different people, and I was the only one who knew it.

In front of others he was the person I fell in love with. There were times when I still did love him, but these times seemed few and far between. I often wished that things would go back to the way they used to be, back to the time when he did love me. I didn't know what had changed, or what I had done to make him stop. If only I could be the person he wanted me to be then he would love me again. The problem was that I didn't know what kind of person that was. Every time I thought I was doing the right thing, it turned out to be wrong.

'You stupid bloody bitch, can't you ever do anything right?'

Each time Dean said this to me I felt more and more worthless. My self-esteem plummeted. I wasn't allowed to wear make-up or nice clothes. I didn't feel good about myself at all any more, and there was nothing I could do to make myself feel any better, except get high.

I walked around with my eyes to the ground; I no longer looked at anyone. If a man smiled at me and Dean noticed there was hell to pay. I wasn't allowed to talk to anyone except the drug dealers I had to see. These were the only people Dean permitted me to speak to, and even then he accused me of sleeping with them.

The violence escalated and soon became a daily ritual. The guys had stopped coming around. Dean had told them not to – apparently, I made eyes at them all. According to Dean I wanted to sleep with everyone I ever met.

It became a common occurrence every morning that Dean awoke me with a punch to the head. He had not hit me in the face for a long time; he didn't want to leave bruises that people would see. He did not want people to think he was anything but the loving partner he pretended to be.

He continued to force himself on me. One day I suggested that he relieve himself because I wasn't in the mood. He looked at me, disgusted, how dare I suggest such a thing.

'That's what you're here for.' According to him he owned me and he could use me any way he pleased. I think he actually gained more pleasure through my kicking and screaming. He liked the control. He liked the power he had over me and he knew there was nothing I could do about it. Sometimes he tied me up so I couldn't move and if I screamed too loud he gagged me. He would rape me over and over again. It didn't matter where and it didn't make any difference if Kate was in the room.

'Please, Dean, not in front of Kate. Please.' I would beg him, tears stinging my eyes.

'This is all you fuckin' females are good for. She might as well see it and get used to it early.'

Kate's screams would match my own. If I could just keep looking at her, no matter what else was happening. As long as I could see her face I could block out the pain, as long as I concerned myself with her cries I no longer heard my own.

After pleasuring himself Dean would always leave. I didn't know where he went and I didn't care, just as long as he left me alone.

Bleeding, torn and broken, it was a while before I could move. Kate would crawl over to me and hug me, resulting in a burst of fresh tears. I didn't feel sorry for myself; it was my daughter I felt for. The things she was seeing no-one should ever have to see. And I was powerless to stop it, unable to protect her.

I was raised in the Catholic faith, I went to a Catholic

school and once I believed in God. My faith had now dwindled to the point of non-existence. God had forsaken me. My prayers always went unanswered; this God who was supposed to love me was letting me die. A slow, painful and lonely death. I had trouble believing that a God so powerful and so full of love could let this happen. How could he let people suffer the way he did?

I often fantasised about finally reaching heaven and giving this God a good, swift kick in the balls.

It was then I realised I was no longer on God's turf. This was an evil place and it was the devil who was pulling my strings, like I was a puppet in his own sick game.

I was so naive I didn't know that what Dean was doing to me was a crime. I knew rape was a crime, but I didn't know you could be raped by your own partner. I just thought this was the way it was and couldn't understand why nobody had warned me. Why had I not been told that if your man wanted you, demanded you, that you had to be willing to give yourself to him? Why weren't other women as unhappy about this arrangement as I was? I hated being a woman.

Dean's parents were divorced when he was in his early teens and he had two younger brothers. They were raised in the same terrible neighbourhood I was now wasting away in. Their mother was a lovely woman and was not in this situation through choice, but rather through circumstance. She had tried unsuccessfully to instil in her sons the high moral standards she herself lived by.

Dean's father, on the other hand, was a domineering male.

'Women belong in the kitchen barefoot and pregnant,' was his attitude.

When I was heavily pregnant with Kate he had informed me that if the baby was a girl he would want nothing to do with her. Girls were not worth anything in his eyes. It was no wonder his sons held women in such little regard.

I had never heard people talk this way. My parents had always told me that I could do and be anything I wanted, that it made no difference what sex I was. Feminism had not made it to this small pocket of the world. It was a man's domain and, as far as they were concerned, they owned your mind, body and soul.

You only had to take a walk to see that women were treated like second-class citizens in our neighbourhood. It was not a fun place to be. It wasn't unusual to hear bloodcurdling screams escaping from behind closed doors and you knew another woman was suffering the same sad existence as you.

The police rarely helped and I had noticed that for quite a few women they often made matters worse. They would arrest the man and lock him up in the police cells for a few hours to calm him down. What the police did not realise was that once these men were free to go they were pretty pissed off with the women who had put them there. Their anger grew after sitting locked in a cell, simmering away, thinking up new ways they could execute their vicious revenge.

It is hard to know what to do to save yourself when your options are limited. I was in a no-win situation. I wasn't sure how long I could survive the hell I was currently living, yet I was scared to call the people who should have been available for my protection.

Kate and I were enjoying our time together while Dean had disappeared, as he normally did on payday. We had taken a trip into town to do our usual rounds of the various charities to enable me to pay some bills and eat. I hated doing this and it made me feel terrible, but it was better than starving.

I had been to Social Security to see if there was a way they could pay the money into my bank account instead of Dean's.

'I am terribly sorry but that is not possible.' These were not sympathetic people. Kate was screaming because I had nothing to give her. And all this person could say was I'm terribly sorry.

'So you are telling me that because I am a woman you won't pay me? Even though I am the one who looks after and feeds the baby – when there is food to give her, that is.'

'Like I said, I am terribly sorry.' This woman was driving me seriously mad, all she could do was say sorry, and my daughter was shrieking in my ear.

'Okay,' I said, trying hard to control my temper. 'How about you take my daughter home and feed her, because I can't.' I was now fighting back tears.

'I am sorry but there is nothing I can do.'

So it was official – being a woman sucks, big-time. I was living with a man so it was up to him to support us, but what the hell do you do when he refuses? The money paid to us was to help look after Kate, not Dean, and he still had his criminal dealings on the side. No amount was ever enough, and he wasn't in the least bit concerned that he was taking food out of his own daughter's mouth.

Kate and I were playing with some coloured wooden blocks on the lounge room floor. I carefully stacked the blocks one on top of the other and watched as Kate knocked them over. I loved the sound of her laugh as the block tower came tumbling down; it was music to my ears and something I did not hear often enough. She would sit there clapping her little hands, laughing hysterically. She was the only thing that brought a smile to my face these days. When Dean was not at home it gave us both the chance to relax a little. We could smile and we could laugh – something not permitted at other times. Happiness came at a price. The price was set by Dean and it was very high.

BANG.

All of a sudden the heavy wooden front door came

flying through the house. There was no formal entryway; the front door opened straight into the lounge room. The door flew past us so close I felt the breeze in its wake. Kate's happy laughter turned quickly into shocked tears. I heard myself scream and quickly scooped Kate into my arms.

'What the fuck is going on in here?' Dean was standing where the front door once was, looking every bit like the Terminator; it was a terrifying sight.

'Nothing, Dean. Nothing is going on.' I was backing slowly up to the wall behind me, Kate still crying in my arms.

'Bullshit.' He came charging towards us, rage in his eyes. He pulled the screaming Kate from me and threw her on the couch.

'No!' I screamed, lunging towards her. Dean stopped me short, throwing me to the floor like a ragdoll. My head hit the ground painfully hard.

'You bitch.' Dean planted a heavy foot in my ribs, before reaching down and pulling me up by the hair. I was sobbing hard, hurting all over. He turned me around so I could see Kate. Her face was red from crying, tears were streaming down her little puffy cheeks, her eyes pleading with me to pick her up and keep her safe.

'She's the only thing that matters to you, isn't she?' Dean growled.

He punched me hard in the stomach, still holding me firmly by the hair with his other hand. He then picked me up and threw me as hard as he could into the wall: I crashed through the plasterboard, landing on the other side. That was the last thing I remember.

When I came to, I was lying on the floor in the bedroom surrounded by pieces of the wall I had plunged through. I moaned and tried unsuccessfully to move. The pain was intense and covered my entire body. How long had I been lying there unconscious – was it only a few minutes, or had it been hours? I didn't know.

A sudden thought entered my head. Oh no, where was Kate? I moaned again as I forced myself to roll over, pain shooting through every part of me.

'Katie. Katie, where are you?' The house was silent. I used all my strength to haul myself to my hands and knees, painfully, slowly.

'Katie. Katie, it's Mummy. Katie.' My vision blurred as tears started to well up in my eyes, not only from the pain but also out of concern for my missing baby. I was beginning to panic.

'Please, God, don't let him have hurt her. Please.'

As I pulled myself into the lounge room I saw Kate on the couch. She wasn't moving.

'Oh my God, no, Katie,' I sobbed, trying to move faster, cursing myself for not being able to.

'Katie, Kate.' I said her name over and over, as I inched my way to her, willing her to hear me. 'Katie, please wake up.'

It seemed to take an eternity before I finally got to her.

She was so still. I placed my hand, covered with dried blood, gently on her forehead. I watched as her big, baby-blue eyes slowly opened.

'Mum, Mum.' I was so relieved I covered her little face with a million kisses. Dean was right – she was all I cared about and I didn't know what I would do without her. If he ever hurt my baby I knew I would kill him.

I was covered with cuts and scratches; huge black bruises began to appear all over me. My back was a complete mess and probably needed a few stitches in some places, but I refused medical treatment. I did not want to explain it all again; I was far too ashamed.

This time the police were called. I needed the front foor fixed and I was sick of Dean getting away with how he treated us. I was glad when he was arrested that night. He was charged with assault and a court date was set. He was not allowed to come to the house. I had been granted an interim restraining order, which would remain in place until we both attended court.

Dean was not stupid enough to come near us with a restraining order hanging over his head. If he had been, he would have been sent straight to goal. Which I would not have minded in the least.

I had become good friends with the wife of one of the dealers who lived nearby. Fiona was a lot older than me and had lived a very tough life; she had seven children to five different fathers and had not had good relationships with any of them. She had been beaten so badly once that she was admitted to hospital with a broken jaw and various other fractures.

Her current husband, Chris, fathered her two youngest children and was a pussycat. He would never have touched Fiona, I think he was more scared of her. She was tough and took crap from no-one any more.

Fiona was the one person I could talk to. She understood.

'The only person who can help you is you. You have to get smart, Amy; you have to do whatever it takes to survive. You have to be stronger than him.'

'But how, Fiona? How do I beat him?' I didn't know how to – Dean was bigger and stronger. I was weak and barely had enough strength to get through each day.

'You have to get inside his head, figure out how he ticks. You can learn to be as sneaky and as dangerous as he is, Amy. You have to.'

Friday was dubbed ladies' day at the local courthouse. It was a busy day; there were a lot of women trying to obtain restraining orders against violent partners. The waiting rooms were crammed with women from all walks of life and there were dozens of noisy snot-nosed kids running up and down the corridors. It was an unsettling sight – so many women and children in the same predicament.

I was waiting at one end of the courthouse with Kate singing to herself in the stroller. I was caught off guard when Dean entered the large room, his eyes burning into me like laser beams. He was dressed in a suit, in contrast to most of the male scum in the building who were dressed in dirty jeans and T-shirts with AC/DC or Metallica emblems. Of course Dean had to be there looking like a god. I should not have expected anything less.

I had tried to look as presentable as I could, yet the only clothes I had were falling off me because of the amount of weight I had shed. I looked down at Kate who looked as bad as I did. Her jumpsuits had grown too small, her little toes were poking out through holes. I wanted to cry.

When Kate had been a couple of months old I had bought her a little dress. It only cost $10 and was the first thing I had purchased for her. When I had returned home with the dress Dean hit me. She had enough. Why was I spending money on her? Dean expected me to only use the hand-me-downs others had given us.

Once inside the courtroom Dean's behaviour was that of the blameless, wronged partner. As usual, everything was my fault.

'Your honour, she is crazy. When she loses control I have no choice other than to defend myself.'

I wanted to hurl myself at him, the bastard. He was putting on an Oscar-winning performance. It was such a good show the magistrate believed every word that came out of his mouth.

'Young lady,' the magistrate turned to address me.

'Have you considered the fact that you may be suffering from postnatal depression? That could be the reason for your irrational behaviour.'

Fantastic! I couldn't believe this. Now I wanted to hurl myself at the bloody magistrate. I felt like showing them just how irrational I could be.

'I suggest, miss,' he continued, 'that you both go home and you do what you are told.'

No restraining order was granted. I felt sick to the stomach. They were going to let him kill me. They were supposed to help me and they were going to let him take me home and kill me.

Chapter 3

I remained lost in my own misery and self-pity. Dean became more cruel and vicious than he had been in the past. Fiona was right – nobody was going to help me. The magistrate had provided Dean with the ammunition he needed to continue his rampage. If the magistrate said I was crazy then I must be. Dean constantly threw this in my face. Sometimes, I felt like I actually was crazy.

I no longer knew who I was. I had been shaped and moulded like a piece of Play-Doh to fit into Dean's insane fantasy. I no longer controlled my thoughts or feelings – Dean did. I no longer controlled anything.

Dean started making me go to pawnshops to hock the stolen goods he acquired most nights. The police had started checking pawnshop records and every time a break and enter occurred they would go through the books to see if any of the items had been sold. Dean did not want his own name on the books, but mine was fine. If I were caught, who would care? I didn't want to do it but knew I could not refuse.

Dean didn't have a driver's licence, so I used to have to drive him and his brother to the pawnshops if the things could not be traded for drugs. The last time this happened they were caught. There were dozens of undercover cops patrolling the area. I stood across the road watching as Dean and his brother Jamie walked into the shop with a couple of power saws.

The owner of the shop made them go out onto the footpath to start the saws: he must have known they were stolen. As soon as Dean started them up, plain-clothes police came from everywhere.

There was a block of public toilets directly behind me so I ran to them. One of the policemen bolted across the road after me, reaching me before I got to the toilet block. He grabbed hold of my arm and spun me around to face him.

'I think you should come with me.' He didn't look much older than I was; dressed in baggy jeans and a gang jacket, he looked like a rapper.

'No. I haven't done anything wrong,' I said, trying to twist myself out of his grasp.

'You're with them, aren't you.' It was more a statement than a question; he turned around and pointed to the boys who were being escorted across the road, surrounded by more rapper police.

'Yes, but I didn't do anything. They made me drive them.'

'Oh really. And you don't have a brain of your own?' If only he realised how true that was.

'But you don't understand.' I wished he would let me go.

'I understand perfectly, Miss Innocent.' He was being sarcastic now.

Dean had the car keys so I wasn't able to drive off and leave them there if anything did happen. The police had now surrounded my car and were pulling the seats out. A large crowd had gathered in the car park to watch what was happening. I was so embarrassed. The rapper policeman who had caught up with me dragged me over there. They were pulling everything out of my car; they even tipped my handbag upside down, its contents spilling over the ground.

'Where are the drugs?' This question was directed at me by one of the cops holding on to Dean.

'What drugs?' I played dumb. If they thought I was actually going to tell them they were sadly mistaken.

'The drugs you have stashed in your car.' This was said slowly, as if I was three years old and didn't understand the question the first time.

'I told you, there are no drugs.' They had completely emptied the car and hadn't found them yet. Did they really think I was that stupid? If I told them, my life wouldn't be worth living. Dean would see to that.

The boys were taken to the station. Apparently there was nothing the police could hold me for, although

I thought I would have been charged as an accessory or something. I was shitting myself. I found out later the reason they couldn't hold me was because I was not actually in possession of the stolen goods, which was why they had searched the car. Had they found the drugs I would have gone for that, charged with possession, because it was my car.

I was left standing in the parking lot with my empty car. They hadn't even put the seats back in. Everything that had been inside was now spread all over the car park. The crowd had not dispersed even though most of the excitement was over. I think they were now mostly interested in how I was going to rectify this problem on my own.

This was the last time Dean tried to hock anything himself. I was always scared that I was going to get caught, though miraculously I never did. I don't know why – some of the things were obviously stolen and even had engravings identifying where they came from. I had to hock a television and video player once with the name of a local school engraved for all to see. Yet somehow they never came after me.

Birth control no longer worked because I was sick all the time. I vomited constantly and was becoming weaker and weaker. I weighed only 43 kilos, and was beginning to look like a walking skeleton. I remembered a cartoon that was on TV not too many years ago. I think it was called 'He-Man' and I was turning into his adversary, Skeletor. It was difficult to keep anything down; I would force myself to eat a piece of dry toast every morning, unsuccessfully. Dean would yell at me for wasting food.

By the time Kate was twelve months old I had fallen pregnant three times. I did not tell Dean. I didn't want any more kids to live this life – it was not a life they deserved. I had always been against abortions and each time cried for days afterwards. Dean was under the impression the regular hospital visits were to find out what was making me so sick.

My local doctor confirmed the pregnancies. I think he knew, without my having to say so, how unstable my situation was. Dr Landers quite often commented on my appearance. He gave me appetite stimulants, which unfortunately did not work. As with the pill, these would not stay down. Dr Landers referred me to a gynaecologist each time to arrange the terminations.

I hated walking into the hospital on the date scheduled for the minor surgery. I was sure everyone knew what I was doing there and that they were all cursing me for my own stupidity. I would sit in the blue hospital gown, cap and booties waiting for my name to be called. I had read horror stories about abortions. Some of the stories involved the termination being done while you were awake and you were able to hear all the horrifying noises. Some stories told of women being butchered by backyard

Doctor Jekylls, using utensils such as knitting needles. If they did not die through infection they were left sterile, their bodies unable to carry another child. I remembered being made to watch a video in high school on the subject. It was very disturbing and resulted in many girls, including myself, running from the classroom in tears.

Fortunately, things had changed a great deal. Although it was still illegal, you were at least able to have the procedure done in a hygienic environment by someone qualified to do such a job. I was so relieved the first time, when I was told the operation would be done under a general anaesthetic. I did not want to be awake.

I cried for my lost babies. I would never lay eyes on their perfect little faces. I would never hold them, I would never hear them call me Mum, I would never know if they were boys or girls and I was so guilty I could barely stand it.

I prayed to God, hoping he would understand and not send me straight to hell. I prayed that he would look after my precious little ones until we could one day be reunited. They were better off playing in God's garden. They were the lucky ones. Sometimes I see them in my dreams, these little Kate look-alikes, running and laughing, calling me in happy, carefree voices, willing me to join them in their safe playground. Many times I wanted to join them, to give up and join them in happiness, without a care in the world. I often wake up from these dreams calling to them, wanting them to come back, their faces slowly fading from view, their hands waving goodbye.

I often wondered that if our eyes were windows to our soul, could people see the pain hidden behind mine? If they looked hard enough, did they see?

When we had no money I had to get drugs on credit, or tika as it was called in the drug business. This was not always an easy thing to do, especially if you already owed money. This was where knowing a lot of dealers came in handy. It wasn't unusual to have a tika bill of up to $100 a week, then when you paid it you had no money to buy more; it was a vicious circle. If a dealer had a lot of stuff he didn't mind giving it to you, but if he was running low there was no way he was going to give you any without the money up-front.

Marijuana was double the price of gold per ounce. You could buy a gram for $20, which didn't go very far. The more you bought the cheaper it was, though not many people could afford to buy it in larger quantities. Prices fluctuated depending on how many busts had occurred in the area. An ounce of pot was known to go for no less than $600 if the drug squads had been busy. When there was more available you could pick up an ounce for around $350 dollars. Speed was more expensive at $60 a hit.

Glen was our main man; he supplied the whole area with

drugs of all descriptions. His parents lived nearby and they sold a lot for him. It was a really weird scenario, going to buy drugs from people who looked like your grandparents.

Glen made a killing. He updated his brand new Commodore every twelve months and he had a speedboat, two Harley-Davidsons and a quad runner. All this and he lived in government housing paying $40 a week rent. It wasn't hard to see the attraction that dealing drugs had for so many people. Glen got rich by ruining other people's lives.

The dealers near us never got busted. Glen had the police in his pocket. A lot of the stuff he sold came directly from the cops – they busted someone else and didn't account for all of it in their paperwork. The excess was then passed on to Glen for a very reasonable price.

Glen would turn up at his parents' place with garbage bags filled to overflowing with pot. He would spend hours dividing it up; this was the best time to score. Quite often I would go over there while Glen had the drugs spread all over his parents' kitchen table.

'Amy, how are you today?' He was always a happy guy and was always off his face. I wondered if he was this happy if he wasn't high. Probably not, coming down was the worst; especially coming down from what he was on.

'Not too bad, Glen, how are you?'

'That prick of a man of yours still beating you up?' Glen didn't like Dean; he wasn't a woman-basher and despised anyone who was. Actually he despised most of the men in our area, but he needed their money so did little to prevent what was going on.

'Yeah, but it's nothing I can't handle.' I didn't see the point in whingeing to him.

'Well, put out your hands.' I don't know if he felt sorry for me or not, but I would cup my hands and he would fill them up with as much dope as he could without it falling out all over the place. All this for $20, which was three times the amount you normally got for that kind of money. I thanked him and headed for the front door.

'Hey, Amy, I like you. If I were you I would leave that bastard.'

It sounded so simple – why hadn't I thought of that before? Just leave, get Kate and leave.

That evening I boldly announced my intentions while I had the courage to do so.

'I'm leaving.' Wow, how easy was that? Two simple words and I had said them.

'You really think I will let you do that?' Dean was sitting in front of the television watching 'Sportsweek'. He didn't look at me as he spoke.

I didn't know what to say. My courage had gone as quickly as it had come. No, I really didn't think he would let me leave.

'Okay, off you go then. Let's see how far you get. You

know you will never survive without me. You're too stupid to do anything for yourself.'

I was dumbstruck. He was letting me go and it all seemed a little too easy. I ran into the hallway and headed for the bedroom. Kate was having an afternoon nap, so I packed as many of my own clothes as I could fit into the Adidas sports bag that was lying on the floor. I then went into Kate's room and packed the small amount of belongings she had. I picked her up, not worrying that I had woken her.

I grabbed the bags and headed for the door. Dean had still not moved from his television program.

'You're making a big mistake, Amy.' This was all he said as I hurried out the door towards the car.

I threw the bags in the back seat and strapped Kate into her sheepskin-covered car seat. I then raced around to the driver's side and jumped in behind the wheel. I started the car, half-expecting Dean to come bounding down the front steps and drag me back into the house. I reversed the Mazda out the driveway, my legs shaking, making it extremely difficult to keep my foot on the clutch. I felt sick and thought I might throw up.

I drove out of the street as fast as I could, still expecting Dean to somehow stop me. There was no sign of him as I looked in the rear-vision mirror. I breathed a sigh of relief and edged my way closer to the border of this gloomy neighbourhood. I reached the main road where the murkiness ended and the colour began.

As I made my way further into the land of the living, I saw children laughing and playing on their manicured bright green lawns. It made a distinct change from the thirteen-year-olds who walked around Clairvale with cans of Jim Beam, talking in profanities as though this was the norm. The police would pick up five-year-olds who were smashing letterboxes and deliver them back to uncaring parents. These are the kids that scare you at school; these are the kids who learn to terrorise the innocent from a very young age.

I made my way toward my most favourite place in the world, the mountain I loved so much. I drove down the highway as fast as I could, the mountain getting closer. I did not feel free yet, and I wouldn't until I reached my parents who I knew would take Kate and me in. They would not refuse me help if it were needed.

I reached my destination with a heavy heart. What would I tell them? Would they be disappointed in me?

My mother came to the front door and I ran to her as I had done when I was a child. I flung myself into her outstretched arms and held on to her, never wanting to let go. Wanting her to keep me safe from everything, just like she always had done. No matter how much I had let her down in the past I knew she would always love me.

Kate was still asleep in the car because I had interrupted her much-needed afternoon nap. Mum gently pulled her from the seat and took her inside while I grabbed the bags.

Once inside I felt safe. For the first time in a long time, I was safe. My father hugged me with the old familiar bear hug I remembered so well and missed so much.

'What's happened to you, girl? You're skin and bone. Don't worry, we'll fatten you up.' He took Kate and sat with her, bouncing her on his knee.

I could not tell them everything that had happened, it would have hurt them too much. So I kept it simple.

'We know you're not happy, Amy. It doesn't take a genius to figure it out.'

It had been such a long time since I had seen them. Kate had only been a tiny baby the last time. Mum always knew how I felt; we had always had a special bond. From the time I was little we had been very close. The teenage years of confusion and rebellion, however, had made us drift apart.

'So could we stay for a while, Mum? Just until I find a place.' I was practically begging her, I was sure she could hear the desperation in my voice.

'Of course you can. We would never turn you away, Amy, you know that.'

They had always been so good to me and I wondered if I would ever be able to repay them for all they had done and would continue to do.

My two younger sisters still lived at home and were surprised to see us when they arrived from school. Zoe and Brandie were close in age, only eighteen months apart. I was older than Zoe by almost two years and had always felt like the odd one out growing up. They had so many things in common and played together all the time. The three of us each had our own little quirks. I was the miserable one, Zoe the happy one and Brandie was the cute one. Brandie always managed to get her own way and had wrapped my father around her little finger. I think it came with being the youngest.

They both loved their little niece to bits, singing songs to her and telling her stories. They played games with her and tickled her so much her face would turn a light shade of purple. Kate had never received so much attention and seemed to enjoy it very much.

Both girls nagged Mum to let them stay home from school so they could spend more time with Kate. Mum was not going to accommodate their wishes easily and both girls trudged off to school the next morning with sulky looks on their faces. Kate waved them bye-bye.

After a few days I began to eat normally again. Dad practically force-fed me with anything fattening he could find. Every day he would get 2 litres of caramel milk from the milkman for me because he knew I liked it. He would also get lots of yoghurt tubs for Kate. He spoilt us both rotten. It had been a long time since anyone had spoilt me, and I was grateful.

Mum would come home from work with all sorts of new things for Kate. There were the cutest little outfits and shoes, toys and treats. When Mum would show her the things she bought for her, Kate would clap her hands and laugh hysterically, bringing smiles to our faces.

Kate was beginning to talk and had been walking for months. She took her first steps at nine months of age, wanting to chase a bird that had been in the yard.

She called my parents Oma and Opa because my mother was Dutch. All day long she would follow my father, chatting incessantly.

'Opa, Opa. Look,' she would call, and pretend to stand on her head, her feet never leaving the ground. She would just bend over and put her head on the floor. She liked to do all sorts of tricks for her beloved Opa.

I had never seen my little daughter so happy and full of life. I felt terrible for keeping her away from the grandparents who adored her and who she now loved very much.

For the first time since Kate was born I got to sleep in. Dad would get up with her in the morning and switch on the cartoons. Dad had always been a big cartoon fan – when we were kids he would practically be falling all over the floor from laughing at something Fred Flintstone or the Roadrunner had done. I would wake up to the sound of them both laughing in the lounge room, Kate sitting on Dad's knee.

I had been to Social Security and had applied for the Sole Parent's pension; I also applied for government housing, as I would not have been able to afford private rent on the pension.

Dean had rung the house a couple of times, resulting in my father hanging up on him, which I knew would have made Dean ropeable. He didn't like people hanging up on him. He considered himself to be a very important person.

'Something for you.' Dad handed me some mail. 'Looks like Dean's writing.'

It was. I held onto it for the longest time, scared to open it. Not knowing what was inside. I stared at it with so much concentration you would have thought I had X-ray vision. I slowly turned the yellow envelope over, taking a deep breath before ripping the top open and removing the letter that was inside. I opened the roughly folded paper and started to read its contents.

Dean was his usual charming self. He called me a bitch, and said that I would never escape him. He ordered me to 'get your arse here now' or he'd rip my 'fuckin' head off'. If I didn't do as he said he threatened to kill my family. Reminding me that he knew where they lived, he pointedly asked me whether I knew how horrible it would be to burn to death. He was furious that my father had hung up on him and warned that if he did it again he'd kill him. He ended the letter 'I am your worst fucking nightmare.'

I finished the letter and stuffed it quickly back into the envelope; I didn't want Dad to see it. I sat staring out the window, wondering what to do now. I knew I should take Dean's threats seriously. I knew better than anyone what he was capable of. And he was capable of following his threats through, that much I was sure of. I would never forgive myself if Dean hurt my family.

'Everything all right?' Dad was standing in front of me. 'Aim? I said is everything all right?'

Dad was worried, I could tell, but I just sat there. I didn't know what to say; I didn't know what to do. I just sat there staring straight through him, lost in my thoughts.

'Dad, I have to go back. Please don't ask me why. Just trust me.' I couldn't cry. I wanted to, but I couldn't. I wanted to jump up and scream. I wanted Dad to take me away and never have to let me go through any of this again. I was nineteen years old and had been through enough.

I wished I could go back to being a little girl, when I would climb up on Dad's knee, just as Kate did now. When Dad would stroke my hair and make everything better, or cover a cut knee with a Band-Aid and give me a jelly bean to stop the tears.

Nothing would be that easy again. My parents were no longer able to protect me from danger. Dean had me right where he wanted me. He thrived on my fear. But why had it taken him so long? Why had he not demanded me back before this?

I had been here for two months, and he knew where I was the entire time. Why did he wait?

In the two months I had gained five kilos, and was no longer sick every day. Dad made sure I ate every hearty mouthful he made for me. He refused to let me leave the table without my wiping my plate clean. I hated this when I was growing up. But now I could see it was done out of love, and that he cared for me deeply – with all the stength and passion that a parent has for their child. I only realised how strong the parent–child bond is since having Kate. It is a connection that can never be broken, not through time nor space.

I was about to break my parents' hearts again and could barely stand it. My own heart had already broken; shattered into a million tiny pieces and I didn't care if I ever felt anything again. I didn't want to feel. My heart would never mend.

The next morning all of the lovely things that had been bought for Kate were packed in the car, together with my own things. Mum hugged me so tight I thought I might break and Dad didn't want to let me go. They didn't understand. How could they? I had offered no explanation as to my sudden departure. All I had said was, 'Trust me.'

Kate kissed Opa on the cheek and traced her finger along the tracks of Oma's tears. As I strapped her into the car seat she blew them a kiss and yelled out.

'Lub you.'

I tried hard to fight back my own tears. I did not want to cry in front of them – if I had they would have tried to stop me. I couldn't let them do that, for their own sake. I loved them too much.

As I watched them grow smaller in the rear-vision mirror I let the tears fall silently down my face, betraying me. My heart had not grown as cold as I had hoped. I still felt.

Chapter 4

As I left behind the land of the living, my mountain and everything that was dear to me, I was unsure what awaited me. I knew revenge would be in Dean's plans, but what concerned me was the unknown. I had been on the wrong side of Dean's fist plenty of times; it wasn't the pain that scared me any more. The mind games were far more dangerous than any physical suffering I had endured. Cuts and bruises healed in time but the mind had its own agenda and was not going to heal itself.

I drove slowly; there was no hurry. I made the hour-long drive stretch to two – I didn't even reach the speed limit, which was unusual for me. I had been known to be a bit of a leadfoot, and had been pulled over for speeding a number of times.

As I drew closer, the butterflies began to wreak havoc in my churning belly; it was as though they would force their way out of my body like the alien Sigourney Weaver battled in the movies.

I drove into the driveway and stopped the car, forcing myself to open the door and hop out. There was as yet no sign of Dean. I thought he would have come out as soon as he noticed the car. Kate was sleeping so I decided to leave her there and face Dean on my own first. If there was going to be trouble, and I was sure there would be, I wanted Kate as far away as possible. I was grateful she had not woken up.

I entered the house and stood in the doorway, not wanting to proceed any further. There was still no sign of Dean. I took slow steps down the hallway and heard the sound of the shower turn off in the bathroom. I stopped, frozen, my hands clammy, fear taking hold. The bathroom door opened and Dean stepped out in a plume of steam with a towel wrapped around his waist.

He took a couple of steps toward me and embraced me tightly. I almost passed out from shock. What was he doing? This was not what I had expected.

'Don't ever leave me again.' It was not a threat, it was more a heartfelt plea. What the hell was going on?

'I love you so much I can't live without you.' He still had not let me go.

I couldn't speak; this was the Dean I had not seen in such a long time. This was the side of him I had yearned for, the loving Dean. The Dean I loved.

Maybe he realised how serious I was this time. Maybe

he realised he couldn't treat me the way he had because I would not put up with it. Maybe he realised I wasn't as stupid and helpless as he first thought. Maybe things were going to be different.

He gently picked me up and took me into the bedroom, laying me on the bed. He slowly undressed me, kissing every part of my body, lingering on the scars made by his anger.

'I am so sorry,' he whispered over and over again. 'Please forgive me.'

'Don't hurt me again, Dean.' I whispered back.

'Never, Amy. I promise never again.'

He made love to me passionately, sensitively, the way he used to. I wanted to scream out in happiness. My Dean was back. As long as he was sorry, I was willing to forgive him. As long as he didn't go back to his old ways I could love him again.

It had been over twelve months since he had treated me this way. Over twelve months since he had loved me. I wanted Kate to grow up with both parents just as I had done. If we could make this work, surely she would be better off.

Kate was still sleeping when I went to the car to get her. I felt as peaceful as she looked; I smiled as I lifted her limp body out of the car seat.

'Daddy's better,' I quietly whispered in her ear, careful not to wake her.

I took her inside while Dean went to the car to collect

the belongings that we had taken, plus the many extras my parents had supplied us with.

'Honey?' Wow, I nearly fell off my chair. What had happened to the endearing 'shithead' epithet I had become so very used to? All I could do was look at him.

'I'll cook you the best dinner you've ever had. Steak all right?' Shit, he really was after forgiveness. Who the hell was this stranger?

'Um. Steak's fine, Dean. Thanks.' I was still in rather a shocked state; I was not used to these niceties from him.

I liked it; it was a refreshing change. I had been so worried that he was going to be vicious on my return. I thought it was going to be worse than it ever had been. I had not forgotten about the nasty letter that had been sent to Mum and Dad's. How could I forget such a thing? But as long as Dean was being nice I didn't want to make waves. I didn't want to be the cause of his anger returning. As long as everything stayed like this I was safe, my family was safe and Kate was safe. That was all I cared about.

That night nothing was expected of me. Dean placed none of his usual demands on me. It was a quiet and uneventful night. Dean made Kate's dinner and even cleaned up after her. She loved to feed herself, which could be a very messy procedure, spaghetti everywhere – she seemed to really enjoy placing the full bowl on top of her head. She thought it was very funny, and couldn't see why I found no humour in this. On an average day she needed several baths to keep her clean. She was always covering herself with food.

Dean bathed her and had her tucked away in bed by six o'clock. I think she was happy to be at home in her own bed for there was not a single peep out of her. She did not normally go down so easily.

Once he had done this Dean started on our dinner while I sat on the couch with the Bryce Courtenay book *The Power of One*. I loved this book and had read it many times. I never got sick of it. There were some books I could read over and over again – another favourite was Barbara Erskine's *Child of the Phoenix*. I loved these kinds of stories; they made me feel so much better about my own life. If I could put myself in their shoes for a while, my situation never seemed quite so bad. Books were my way out, my escape to another world, another time and another adventure.

'Here you go.' Dean handed me a plate piled with steak, chips, vegies and gravy. It looked good and I was hungry.

'Thanks.' I took the plate and began to devour the meal. Dean had never been the best cook, but this was very nice.

I finished the last mouthful and went to the kitchen to begin tidying up. Men were the messiest cooks, it seemed every dish and utensil had been used in order to make this simple but tasty meal.

'Don't touch anything. Get back out here and finish your book,' Dean called from the lounge room.

'It's okay, Dean. I don't mind – you cooked, so I'll clean up.'

'I said come out here and relax. You're not doing anything tonight.'

Wow. This was different. Even the nice Dean I had known in the beginning didn't look after me this well. Maybe he did have a conscience after all.

'Gee, Dean, I could get used to all this pampering.' I sat back on the couch and picked up my book.

'Good. You deserve it.' He came over and tenderly kissed me on the head before taking himself off to begin the major clean-up that was required in the kitchen.

I still couldn't get over the change in him. It wasn't that I didn't like it, but deep down I wondered how long it would last. I had seen his apologies before, but none like this. I had wished for this for such a long time it made me feel a little uneasy. My wishes were very rarely granted and usually ended with a slap in the face, metaphorically speaking. It didn't matter what it was; no granted wish ever ran smoothly.

I scolded myself for thinking that way. I should just shut up and enjoy it. I had suffered enough; maybe it was time for my dreams to come true. And my greatest wish, my greatest dream, was that our little family could function the way a family should. Through love, not hate. If Dean remained this way my dream could come true.

'Tomorrow I am taking my two favourite girls to the zoo.'

'Really?' I couldn't believe what I was hearing. The zoo? I hadn't been to a zoo since I was a little kid. And since when did Dean take us anywhere?

'Yes, really.'

The next day we were up early and on our way to Sydney on the train. Kate had never been on a train before and was so excited, there was no car seat to strap her into and she liked the freedom; it was very different from the car that she was used to travelling in. Her large blue eyes were opened so wide I thought they might pop right out of her skull. She was taking in all the busy sights and sounds. She jumped up and down on the seat next to the window.

'Look, look.' Her little fingers pointing at something that flew quickly past her with the speed of the train.

It was hard to get her to sit still. She was wearing one of the outfits Mum had bought for her. It was a little pink tracksuit with a bear appliquéd on the front. She also wore a pair of tiny pink and white runners and a white lace headband. Kate had barely any hair; it was not long enough to put in little pigtails. Even though she was normally dressed in girl colours some people had mistaken her for a boy because of her lack of hair. I was glad she now had some headbands, I hoped it would stop the confusion.

I was jealous of little girls of a similar age who had full heads of hair. My Kate was a bit like me in that department: bald as a badger for the first few years of life. She seemed to have more hair when she was born. I had been devastated when it started rubbing off on her little baby pillow.

Kate was fiercely independent for such a small girl. She hated being strapped into the stroller from the time she could walk. 'No!' she would say, with her brow wrinkled into a severe frown and her little arms folded across her chest. She meant business.

Today was no different. Once we were off the train there was no way she was going to get into that cramped stroller.

'C'mon little chicky-babe,' Dean said as he hauled her up onto his shoulders.

'Yay!' she screamed. 'Fun, fun!'

The station was bustling with people all hurrying to get on with their daily activities. We made our way through the crowd to Circular Quay where we waited to catch the ferry that would take us to the other side of the harbour, where Taronga Zoo was located.

Now, if we thought the train thrilled Kate to bits, it was nothing compared to the ear-piercing excitement of the ferry ride. She wanted to stand too close to the safety rails and I was scared she was going to fall in.

'You hold on to her tight, Dean,' I demanded.

'Yes, mother.' He grinned sideways at me.

The zoo was surprisingly busy for a weekday, all tourists visiting the beautiful city of my birth. I was born not too far from here and lived in the city up until the age of five. I can remember bits and pieces of that time long ago. We lived in a block of flats not far from the beach and spent most days playing in the sand and sea. I was a bit of a water baby, which is where Kate got her love of the water. It was hard to keep her away from it; she always managed to find a puddle, even weeks after rain.

Kate was introduced to animals of all descriptions. There were giraffes and monkeys, tigers and snakes. I had read her the story of Noah's Ark. It was her favourite. Every time she wanted a story she would waddle off to get the same book. She knew most of the animals we saw now, and the noises they made. At each enclosure we came to, she would imitate the sounds I had taught her. She made up her own sounds for the ones she didn't know. She walked such a long way I wondered how she could continue; I was beginning to get tired.

'Why don't we find somewhere to sit down for lunch?' I said to Dean, my legs unsure whether they could take another step.

'You reckon you can make Kate sit down long enough?'

We walked back to the toddler playground we had passed a little way back. If Kate didn't want to sit she could play while Dean and I ate the picnic lunch we had brought from home. I knew, though, that if Kate didn't slow down she would be unbearable later. And an overtired one-year-old is not a pretty sight.

Surprisingly, she sat with us and ate the Vegemite

sandwich I had packed for her. She loved Vegemite and ate it by the spoonful from the jar. I don't know how she did that – I like Vegemite too but I couldn't eat it that way.

Dean and I polished off the chicken, lettuce and mayo sandwiches I had made. I was so hungry with all the walking we had done, two sangers just wasn't enough. I was famished.

Kate looked very tired and I managed to coax her into the empty stroller I had been pushing all day. I smothered her in more sunscreen. Although it wasn't a hot day the sun was beaming down on top of us and there was not a cloud to be seen in the bright blue sky. Our jumpers, which had been needed when we began our journey, had been discarded hours ago and were now tied around our waists.

Kate gratefully accepted the bottle filled with apple and blackcurrant juice I offered her and she closed her eyes, drifting off to sleep surrounded by noisy zoo animals and people. Thankfully, this child could sleep through anything.

'Well, I think this would be the perfect time to check out the gift shop,' I said to Dean.

Kate turned into a terror in shops. She wanted to touch everything she saw and screamed when she could not have what she wanted. I had heard an awful lot about the terrible twos but nobody ever mentioned the shocking ones.

It always fascinated me that in shops everything that

little hands would want was always placed at their level, within easy reach. In supermarkets the lollies were always by the register when you were waiting in long queues to be served. Quite smart on the part of the shop owners as parents would purchase these unwanted items just so their child would not make an embarrassing scene. I myself had been guilty of this on more than one occasion. Kids learn to get their own way from such a young age. They really are smarter than we give them credit for.

We walked out of the gift shop with a stuffed kangaroo that was almost the size of Kate and a little T-shirt with most of the animals we had seen and the words '*I've been to Taronga Zoo*' printed on the front. I couldn't wait to see the expression on her face when she saw the kangaroo – I knew she would love it as soon as Dean had picked it up. These things held a special meaning for me; they were the first things Dean had bought for his daughter since she had entered the world. Although I did not remind him of this sad fact – I was just glad that he had.

We bought ourselves an ice-cream each and wandered slowly down the winding path past the animal enclosures to the waiting ferry. It was a pity Kate was asleep; she would miss her favourite part of today's adventure. I was glad for the break, though, and I would not have to worry this time about her falling overboard.

We sat down at the front of the boat that would take us back across the harbour. Dean put his arm around me and I thanked him for the wonderful day.

'Anything for you, my darling.'

Almost two full days had gone off without a hitch. No insults, no smacks in the head. I found myself wondering – not for the first time since yesterday – when it was all likely to end and go back to the way it was. I had trouble believing Dean could have changed for the better in only two months. Although I had also had trouble believing that he could have changed from the nice, loving person he had once been toward me into the monster I had come to know so well.

Dean had never been this nice to me even when we met. He had never called me darling, and he had never been quite so attentive. In the past his apologies for hurting me only consisted of a 'sorry' and maybe, if I was lucky, a flower he had picked from someone else's garden. He had never been one for buying me anything, let alone taking me out. The only outings we ever went on were our nightly criminal escapades. I think I was a little more confused now than I had been before.

I had always been a sceptical person. Maybe it was time for me to change into a more optimistic one. I really should try looking on the bright side more often, try to see the rainbows instead of gloom, always expecting the worst. I had been the same as a child. Gloom followed me like a dark cloud, apart from when I was dancing. I had been given the nickname 'misery guts' from my father when I was a young child. I had never been a morning person and one of my sisters would always get up first thing in the morning and sing happy songs. She would sing songs like 'You Are My Sunshine'. I much preferred 'I Don't Like Mondays'.

We arrived home late in the afternoon, Kate coming to life again on the train ride back. She tightly hugged her new kangaroo friend all the way, squealing when she first saw it. It was an hour-long trip and I kept thinking, thank goodness this kangaroo is not a living, breathing creature. If it had been then it would be no longer. Kate's grip around his neck was so tight it would have squeezed the life right out of him.

The next day we went to Dean's mother's house for lunch while Dean finished off her garden. He was a keen gardener and was very good at it. He could make anything grow without a lot of trouble. Everything he put in the ground thrived; he seemed to have a knack for this. Every Friday night he watched 'Gardening Australia' for tips, hints and tricks. He liked to see what new varieties of flowers and vegetables there were so he could try them.

I myself did not have a green thumb. Everything I tried to grow died. This I inherited from my own mother – she killed flowers too. The only good plant was a plastic plant, was her philosophy, and one I tended to agree with.

Sharon doted on Kate, and Kate loved her Nan very much. Sharon was a teacher's aide in a small Catholic school; she had previously worked as a secretary to the local priest. She attended church when she could but her three sons found church a bore. She was a woman I admired very much. I respected her for all she had done and had tried to do.

Dean was her eldest child and was very intelligent. He had always been in trouble at school, even though he consistently topped his year. Her second son, Jamie, had been a very talented sportsperson and represented Australia in New Zealand for athletics when he was a young teenager. He was also a talented rugby league player, yet just as his brother had done, he fell off the rails somewhere and decided that there was no fun in doing the right thing. Her youngest son, Tim, was only ten years old when Kate was born and still did what his mother told him. I think Sharon held out a lot of hope for Tim. He was her last chance.

Sharon's home was the same as the rest of the government abodes in the area. All these homes looked practically the same. There were only a few different styles: some were freestanding, some were duplexes and some were townhouses.

If you looked carefully you could see what the government's intentions were. These housing estates for low-income earners would have been very nice when first built. The problem seemed to be that together, all these people who relied mostly on welfare to survive – and the majority of the residents were drug addicts and alcoholics – had no respect for something they did not work hard themselves to obtain. Most of the people treated their homes like dumps and used their front and back yards as rubbish tips. It was not unusual to see burnt-out cars in the middle of the roads and old furniture strewn along streets. The frame might be in one place while other pieces of the same bit of junk were found streets away. These people didn't care.

Sharon, on the other hand, took pride in her house and garden. She was in the minority in this area. She did as much as she could do herself with the small amount of money she had to give her family a nice home to live in. The things she could not do herself, Dean often helped her with. It was another world inside, nothing like it was when you stepped out the door and heard the local hoons running amok, polluting the air with their dirty car fumes and blaring loud heavy metal music.

Someone had said to me a long time ago that if a man treated his mother well, then he was a catch. This had been one of the things that had attracted me to Dean. He did a lot for Sharon; when she needed a hand he was always there to help. She didn't drive, so if she needed to go somewhere he was always there to drive her. I don't think she knew he didn't have a driver's licence, although I think she kept her eyes closed to most of the things Dean did. He was her favourite.

Jamie was not well liked within his family, which I found odd, because the things he did were tame compared to what his older brother did.

I had seen on quite a few occasions the consequences when Jamie refused to do what Dean ordered. The poor bloke copped the same wrath I did. You did it or else. Jamie had been left bruised and bloodied from Dean more times than I could count. Dean had to control everyone and everything around him and he worked hard to maintain that control.

Sharon liked to read the stars. When Kate was born she did a chart for her which described her little granddaughter as an independent soul who would need no-one to help her achieve whatever it was that she intended to do in life, an intelligent child who would have a mind of her own. She would be a leader and let others follow her to glory. Only time would tell whether her predictions would come to be.

When I had first met Dean I thought he was Greek or Italian, though his mother's heritage was Irish and his father came from Indian ancestry. Sharon had the strawberry blonde hair and fair colouring that was common in my own family. We burn easily in the hot sun. Kate was lucky, though: with more of her father's colouring she tended to go quite dark in summer and rarely burnt.

'Nan, Nan.' Kate would go running down the driveway to Sharon who would welcome her with a big hug and a kiss. She ran so fast for such a little thing that I was more often than not too scared to watch as she went tearing off, worried she would fall on the concrete and break a bone. She never did, though. She was very sturdy and hardly ever fell over. The times she did lose her balance or trip on unstable ground, she rarely cried. She would just pick herself up, wipe the dirt from her hands and knees and continue as fast as she had begun.

Sharon always had a special treat for Kate, always a small gift that would make Kate very happy. She saw a lot more of Sharon than she did my own parents. It was fine for us to see as much of Dean's family as he pleased. It was mine he did not want to have anything to do with.

Sharon was a very good cook and always had a nice meal waiting for us. After we had eaten Dean went outside and began the gardening work his mother had wanted done while Kate and I helped her clean up. Sharon had told me many times that she thought of me as the daughter she never had. Although, as with my own mother, I could never go to her with my problems as they usually involved her son. I knew she would not believe me and I did not want to be the one to shatter the perfect image of her eldest child. For some reason she never thought Dean was capable of doing wrong, yet assumed Jamie was.

Dean did not show his dark side of himself to his adoring mother. To her he was a gift, to her he meant the world, and if anyone said a word against him it was her wrath they endured. This consisted of a few bad words, nothing more. Sharon was far from a violent woman.

While Dean finished off the work in the garden, Sharon, Kate and I played with the blocks and dolls

Sharon had bought for Kate to keep at her house, so we didn't have to drag toys over there to keep her occupied. Sharon also had a computer program with children's stories on it and a microphone so Kate could chat away and later hear herself on the computer. She got a huge kick out of hearing her own voice come out of the speakers. Sharon and I would be left practically falling around the floor with laughter. This little girl of mine was extremely funny, and I was so proud.

Young Tim also adored his niece and he sat with her for ages, playing. He would softly kick a soccer ball in her direction and let her chase after it and get her to kick it back to him. It almost never made it all the way and usually stopped not far from where she stood. She would then run up to it and try again, resulting in Tim roaring with laughter. He would chase her around and around in circles and I was always grateful as it tired her out. She always slept well on the nights after spending an entire day with her uncle.

Chapter 5

'Hey Aim, go score.'

We had been smoking a lot lately and I was glad because when Dean was stoned Dean was calm. For the most part, anyway. I didn't mind. If he was nice to me and if this helped, then so be it. Drugs were keeping Dean nice and me sane.

I was becoming dependent on it, and so was he. Pot wasn't the only thing we were using. It had been for a while, but lately there were other things. People Dean knew would come over, mostly people he knew from when he had been in gaol or weekend detention. They were tough guys and would bring over pills I didn't even know the names of. I never even bothered to ask – I just swallowed whatever was given to me. I don't know if I didn't ask what I was taking because I didn't want to sound ignorant and stupid, or whether I just didn't care.

I was still worried sometimes about saying the wrong

thing and embarrassing Dean so I usually only spoke when I was spoken to. Even then I think I must have sounded retarded because so much careful thought went into finding an appropriate answer. One that would not get me into trouble.

I took the $20 handed to me and walked around to Fiona's house.

'Fiona, got anything?' I softly called to her through the flywire door.

'Nah, all out, Amy, everyone is.' Fiona opened the creaking door and I stepped inside the four-bedroom house. She had the inside fitted out with amazing furniture. Everything was new and modern; they had the best of everything. New television and video player, stereo with a CD player, all housed in a huge black wall unit that stretched the entire length of the lounge room wall.

Opposite the impressive entertainment system sat a plush grey couch with comfy cushions scattered about. Fiona had an unbelievable collection of kids' videos to amuse her many children when they got too much to handle. When they were rowdy it only meant putting Barney or The Wiggles on and they were happy. They were very pretty kids, dressed in the best clothes, and had the best and most expensive toys, better than anyone else's kids in the street, even the other dealers' kids. Fiona was well liked and made a lot of money from selling drugs.

It's from one extreme to another in these areas. The

majority are poor lower-class people, and dealers make them more miserable, supplying them with drugs and taking money they don't have enough of in the first place. Dealers feed and clothe their kids from the misfortune of others.

Sure, addicts have minds of their own, but when you live day in, day out, in these shit-holes, drug-taking is your only escape out of it for a while. When high you could be anywhere, do anything. Then you start coming down, crashing back to reality and you realise why you got high in the first place. You look at where you are. You look around you. What do you have? Nothing, you haven't got anything.

'Shit. Do you know when you're going to get some?' I asked Fiona.

'Nope. Glen's having some pretty major hassles at the moment, I hear. Apparently it's dry everywhere.'

'Okay. Let me know when you get some, can ya?'

Fiona nodded. Shit. I was a bit worried. What was I going to tell Dean? He would not be a happy man. He didn't like to be straight, and I didn't like him straight. He would probably make me get in the car and drive everywhere trying to find him some.

I tried at the other dealers' houses, each one telling me the same lousy thing.

'Nah, we're out, Amy.'

Shit. Shit. Shit, I thought, walking back home to where Dean waited, probably wondering what was taking me so long.

'Please don't let him be pissed off. Please don't let him be pissed off.' My brain was replaying this thought like a mantra as I reached for the door and turned the handle.

'Well, hurry up. Did you have to grow the shit?' Dean was sitting on the couch. The mull bowl, bong and scissors were on the table ready for the gift I was supposed to bring.

'No-one's got any,' I said, walking slowly towards him.

'Don't bullshit me. One of 'em's got to have some.'

'Dean, really, I tried everyone in the street. It's completely dry. Glen's got some problems getting it.'

'Well, *fuck*,' Dean got up quickly, slamming his hands down on his knees. 'You'll just have to go and find some, won't you?' He was glaring at me, challenging me.

'Why don't you go and find some? You know everyone else better than I do. They're your friends,' I said, glaring back at him as fiercely as he stared at me. I didn't want him to think he could start ordering me around again.

'I just told you to do something. Now do it.' He yelled at me this time.

'No. *You do it*,' I yelled back, standing my ground, determined not to move.

'What?' He walked over to me with a look that didn't suit him at all. It was a mixture of searing anger and disbelief. I don't think he could believe that I had spoken to him like that. I never had before and I kind of scared myself a bit.

I had never been game enough to yell at him before and knew the penalty for refusing his orders. But I was sick of it. I liked how things had been going and I wanted them to stay that way. I didn't want to give in to him. I didn't want him telling me what to do. I wanted a smoke, too. But not that badly.

It would take me hours to go to dealers' houses all over the suburbs. I hated most of them. I hated going into their dingy little hovels. They rarely had their curtains or blinds open and didn't open windows or doors very often to enable the stale smoke to escape. The only time a door opened was to let in another customer, which would result in another smoking session and more smoke filling the already unhealthy air.

One of the places I would have to go was to a friend of Dean's from high school. Andy wasn't a dealer but usually knew where to get on.

The guy was a complete freak. He was a skinny, dumb little bloke. His partner, Justine, was even dumber than he was. She looked like Olive Oyl from 'Popeye', she really did!

They had a son a few months older than Kate and their lounge room walls were covered in pornographic centrefolds from hardcore magazines. There was not a centimetre of wall that did not feature a woman with her legs spread apart, her fingers pulling herself open or inserting something bizarre, like a shower head, into herself. It was disgusting.

They were bringing up a young son in this environment. It astonished me that they didn't think there was anything wrong with it.

They were a strange couple and their son would probably turn out to be yet another woman-basher. A brutal woman-hater just like his father who, mind you, was too stupid to ever get off his scrawny arse and get a job. He believed the government should look after him. He believed it was his right to sit around on the dole and smoke drugs all day. Bash his woman and neglect his child.

Justine used to visit my house and bring food wrapped in the plastic from a sanitary pad because she had run out of cling wrap. She would unwrap the pad packet and feed the cheese, or whatever it happened to be, to her little boy.

The poor kid looked like a child from a Third World country. Just like the kids your heart reaches out to on the World Vision or UNICEF ads, my heart reached out to this little boy. There was snot constantly pouring out of his nose and flies clung to his face. His clothes were filthy and all were too small for him. He was always sick and as a tiny baby was so badly covered with cradle cap I thought it was going to swallow him up and he would be permanently disfigured. It was so thick and stuck into every tiny crevice. His nose, his eyes, every tiny fold. It couldn't be pulled off without removing huge layers of skin with it. It was as though his mother had absolutely no clue about how to look after him.

The more I got to know her, the more I realised this was true. She really didn't have a clue. I had found most things about motherhood were commonsense. The normal, everyday things like bathing and feeding a baby properly I found easy. Nobody had to tell me how to do it. The maternal part of me just took over and it all became second nature.

But she really had no idea and needed to be told how to do everything. She didn't seem to have any commonsense. I felt sorry for her. I felt sorry for her and for the little boy she was trying to raise. The poor kid didn't have a chance.

The more I saw of these people the more I knew I did not want to become like them. They all grew up in these areas; they didn't seem to know what else was out there for them. I did know and I wanted to go back to that side of the world. If Dean continued to punch me in the head all the time, I worried, I would become this silly, lanky woman – and quickly.

I couldn't stand the thought of it. I wasn't going to let Dean intimidate me into submission any longer. Not this time. I wasn't sick any more and felt stronger than ever. Strong enough to fight him, strong enough to realise it was all so wrong and strong enough to stand up for myself.

'I'm not going, Dean. If you want it that badly then you go.' My voice was steady. I was calm. I was doing it.

Dean's face changed very quickly from the confused, angry look into just plain angry. He was starting to look like his head might shoot off his shoulders. It would make a hell of a mess but I found myself wishing for this very remote option to occur. It would be better to clean his brain off the wall, compared to cleaning my own up.

I was sure pain would follow my courageous and foolish steps into the battlefield. Shit, I had brought this on myself. Maybe I should have just shut up.

'Who the fuckin' hell do you think you're talking to?' Dean had an ugly smirk on his face. He wasn't yelling, but I knew he was really pissed off with me. The yelling would come.

'I asked you a fuckin' question.' The ugly smirk was still stretched across his lips and his teeth were tightly gritted together, hard.

I quickly looked down and saw his fists were clenched. Knuckles white.

Shit, what have I done? I could only think, not speak and he wanted an answer.

'I'm sorry, I'll go.' It was the only thing I could think of to say. It just came out. I didn't want to go, but it might get me out of some of the shit I was in for. Thank God Kate was sleeping. I hoped she would stay that way for a while.

'Oh. So you want to go now?' Dean was still speaking through gritted teeth. He reached out and grabbed my arm, pulling me sharply towards him. He lifted me up so that my ear was in line with his mouth. My arm was hurting so much I thought he might break it, although I didn't hear it snap or anything. He had wrenched me into position so hard and fast I was surprised it hadn't broken. I knew there would be huge bruises in a couple of hours.

'Well you're not. I am. You will sit here and think about what I'm going to do to you when I get back.' He began to lower my feet to the ground, but changed his mind and swiftly pulled my arm back up once more.

'Ouch.' I cried out but Dean didn't care.

'And it won't be pretty, sweetheart,' he spat at me before throwing me roughly down on the ground.

He walked into the kitchen and grabbed the car keys from the bench, then stepped over me because I was blocking his path to the front door. He slammed the door loudly on his departure. I expected to hear Kate any minute, although she was used to sleeping through loud noises like that one.

I didn't move. I couldn't move. How could I have been so stupid? Why did I challenge him? Why didn't I just do what he wanted?

'It's not my fault,' I cried softly to myself over and over again. 'It's not my fault, it's not my fault.'

I wanted to believe so badly that it wasn't. A big part of me knew it wasn't. Yet there was another part of me that kept saying, if only I hadn't done this. If only I had done that. If only I just did what I was told. If only I had shut up.

These parts of my brain were always in competition with each other, having their own private battle. Sometimes I felt like I was crazy. I would have arguments with myself, trying to justify something that I had done or something Dean had done.

I would try to justify to myself what the right thing was. Knowing full well what the right thing was and then very successfully talking myself out of it.

Not again. I didn't want to become a slave to Dean's wishes, his desires and sick dreams, again.

'No more. It's not my fault.' I got up off the floor and locked the door.

'Great. What's that going to do?' I said, lifting my good arm into the air in a frustrated gesture. Dean had the car keys, and the house keys were on the same key ring. How could I keep him out if he only had to put the key in the lock and turn it?

I had absolutely no idea what I was going to do. Maybe he wouldn't come back tonight. Maybe once he had got his fix he would forget about me. Maybe if I apologised he wouldn't do anything. Maybe, maybe, maybe, it was always maybe. I never knew exactly what was going to happen, if anything would at all.

I looked around the room and decided that apologising would be by far my best option at this point. I didn't have anything else I could do. He had the car so I was going nowhere. Where would I go? I couldn't go back to my parents' place, or to any family for that matter. What if Dean was serious about his threats to them? I couldn't take that chance. I turned the television on and sat on the couch waiting for Dean's return. My belly churned in the old familiar way when I did not know what to expect. Three hours later Dean returned with the $20 foil that would be lucky to last until the next morning. He was already ripped so wasn't in a hurry to mull up for me or hand it over so that I could.

This was what I was hoping would happen, that he would return too stoned to bother with me. Being stoned mellowed him out considerably. I knew, though, that the same problem would occur tomorrow when what he had bought ran out. I knew I would have to go then.

'Where did you manage to get it from?' I asked, hoping he would tell me so I could go straight there when it was my turn, it would save a lot of time.

'George's,' he answered without so much as a look my way.

'Did you try anywhere else?' I asked.

'Yeah, Hampton's dead. Nothin'.'

George lived in Mossfield which, when the traffic was light, was about a half-hour drive away. If Hampton was out you could be pretty well assured that George would have some. He was to Short Street, Mossfield, what Glen was to the majority of Clairvale. Short Street was a nasty place; I lived there once in a top-floor flat when I first moved out of home. The street was filled with graffiti-covered blocks of units that were the homes of many addicts and immigrants. We called it curry heaven as you could smell people cooking curry as soon as you entered the street. There were other smells as well, indescribable smells. I couldn't tell whether it was some strange food or maybe a decaying body someone had forgotten about.

There were a lot of Asian gangs you had to worry about when going there, although by knowing George you were pretty well covered in the area of protection. It was just a matter of keeping on George's good side. Dean had met him in gaol and I think idolised him. If George said it could be done then it could be done. And you certainly didn't argue with him. He was a big Italian, and you didn't mess with him if you valued your life. He was not an enemy you'd wish for. I had heard the stories. If you didn't pay him what you owed him, George and his cronies would fix you up good and proper. I had heard of one guy who ended up with brain damage after crossing George.

When I first met George he thought I was a cop and didn't sell to me. Ever since then he had been good to me. He always offered me a smoke when I got there as he did with most people he liked. The only problem with George was that he gave out very small deals. You were lucky to get four cones from one of his $20 foils, but who was going to argue or complain? Nobody, so George could do whatever he liked. That was why we only went there when we were desperate.

Sometimes when we were over that way we would drop in to remain sociable. Dean didn't want him to think we only went over to see him when we needed to. Which was entirely true. Dean wasn't so tough when it came to other men. He had to suck up to them or they just might hurt him.

'So do I get some?' I asked timidly, knowing he wasn't going to hand it over unless I begged for it. It wasn't his style.

He threw the small silver package in my direction and went and grabbed the bong, bowl and scissors. I had been worried for nothing; he was too stoned to argue.

As expected, the next day the same argument took place. All the cones had been smoked, the last of course being consumed by Dean. This time, though, I didn't argue when told to go. I just went. There would be no point in fighting with him about something that I would ultimately end up doing anyway. I knew that.

I arrived at George's 45 minutes later and was met with the news that he had just sold his last quarter.

'Shit, George, do you know where I can get some? You know what Dean's like when he doesn't have it.' I practically begged the man, hoping he would have some personal stash he could sell to me. But it wasn't going to happen.

'Sorry, love. Wish I could help ya. Cops have been real busy. Don't you watch the news?'

Yes, I had seen the news. There were dealers being busted left, right and centre. But I had heard all that before and still somebody managed to get hold of something. Not in this case, however. The police were getting everything that was coming in, and they weren't passing it back to the dealers, which was what normally happened. Great – if George or Glen couldn't get hold of it then there was no chance anyone else was going to have any. These two supplied everyone else. The problem was that I had to be the one to break the news to Dean.

Kate had been giving Dean hell. By the time I got back she had been placed in her bedroom. It was impossible to keep her out of the kitchen cupboards. One day I had walked in from hanging the washing out on the line and she was covered in flour. She looked like a little ghost, only her round blue eyes showing. While I was gone she had broken a bottle of pasta sauce and smashed a packet of biscuits. Dean was cleaning the mess off the kitchen floor when I walked through the door.

'Thank Christ you're back. That little bitch has been pissing me off the whole time.'

Excellent, and I was going to break some news that would piss him off even more.

'George is all out too, Dean.' I couldn't tell him any nicer, or let him down any gentler than that.

'No way.' He looked at me in disbelief. 'No fuckin' way,' he yelled, starting to pace the floor. 'Did you try anywhere else?'

'Yeah, I tried Vince's just in case. But he's out as well. Everyone is.' I spoke softly, hoping to calm him down a bit. It didn't work. His fist went slamming into the wall.

'Fuck,' he yelled. 'Gimme the money.'

His cut, bloody hand was outstretched, waiting for me to deposit the $20 note he had given me earlier. I dug it out of my jeans pocket as fast as I could without angering him even more. I didn't want to be seen taking my time.

He snatched the money from me. The large drops of ruby-red blood falling from his hand onto the couch and the carpet seemingly went unnoticed by him. I didn't want to mention the fact that he was making a mess, or the fact that I would be the one to clean it up.

He left, on his way to God knows where. I knew that if there were no drugs to be found he would more than likely return drunk in the middle of the night.

The only time Dean really drank alcohol was when he couldn't get off his face any other way. It was not his drug of choice.

I cleaned up the many thick droplets of dark blood while listening to Kate bang on her bedroom door, wanting to be let out.

With the job finally done Kate was able to come out and we played until it was time to bathe and feed her. Kate loved the bath; I would sit on the closed toilet seat, close to the combined bath and shower in the small cream-coloured room. I had put up bright blue shower curtains that hung down the sides of the tiled bathtub. I would watch Kate splash around in her watery heaven and listen to her sing happy little songs.

She didn't like to get out, and screamed, throwing her legs around as I struggled to lift her slimy body from the water.

For dinner she ate some tuna and mashed potato,

making a huge mess. Most of my time was spent each day cleaning up after her. This one little girl made so much mess and got into so much mischief I needed to have eyes in the back of my head, and an extra pair of arms wouldn't go astray. I couldn't imagine having more than one of these precious little time-wasters and mess-makers. I loved her to death and although there was so much to do for her I couldn't remember what it was like without her.

I couldn't let her outside without watching her closely. The yard was fenced front and back so it seemed very secure and more or less child-proof. Not with Kate around, however; her motto seemed to be 'If there is a will, there is a way.' She had become quite the little fence-climber. The wire fence was twice as high as she was but she would climb up and hoist herself over the top, climbing down the other side. She was impossible, like a tiny Houdini, always disappearing or making other things disappear.

She had a fascination with money. She would take coins that had been left lying around, from anywhere. It didn't matter whose they were or where they were from. If you left them she took them. I found a pile of them in the corner of her bedroom under some stuffed toys. I didn't know what she planned to do with them, but there you go. She did it anyway.

We read stories together and Kate fell asleep at about 6 p.m. Dean had been gone now for four hours and I wondered when he would be back. I hoped it was not going to be tonight. I put Kate to bed in her cosy white timber cot, picked up the book I had started reading a couple of weeks ago and decided to finish it. I only had two hundred pages to go.

I usually liked Stephen King books, but this one was annoying me. I just couldn't get into it, yet I had trouble putting it down. I always had trouble putting books down. Good or bad, it deserved to be finished if it had been started.

So I forged on into the weird world of Mr King and finished the book, still quite disappointed by the whole experience. It just didn't happen for me. I got up from the couch and put the book away, looking at the clock. It was almost midnight and there was still no sign of Dean. I yawned and hoped that he had passed out somewhere and would stay there until morning.

I decided that given the time the odds were good, so I went to bed. I was very tired and my arm still hurt from yesterday. I began to drift off to sleep right away. I love the feeling when you are in between being asleep and awake. Right on the edge of consciousness, when your body feels like it is floating and sinking at the same time. I felt myself slipping into that state, and let it take me off to the world of dreams.

I dreamt of Kate and me at the beach. We were decked out in matching pink bikinis, building sandcastles and laughing in the sun. Swimming in the sea and gliding to shore on the crest of a foamy white wave. Laughing and splashing, jumping and floating.

'Where have all the people gone?' I stood up in the waist-high blue water holding Kate's small hand, her arms swallowed by the yellow floaties around them. The gentle waves started to get stronger, whipping their way around my small waist and almost causing me to lose my balance. I put my hand up to shade my eyes from the sun, to look toward the sandy white shore for all the people who had surrounded us only minutes before. There was no sign of them.

'Fishy,' I heard Kate say in her little-girl voice.

'Pardon, darling?' I asked, trying to find the direction she was looking in.

'Fishy,' she said again.

All of a sudden directly in front of us appeared a huge grey fin. I grabbed hold of Kate's hand and turned, trying to run towards the empty shore. The sun had vanished behind the clouds, giving off an eerie light. I couldn't run away, the heavy water was dragging me back. The shark circled and I felt its sharp teeth around my legs.

'Keep still,' I heard Dean's voice.

What was happening? My legs were hurting.

'Keep still, will ya.' Dean was slurring his words, obviously drunk.

I couldn't move my legs. I was spread out on my stomach, legs apart. I couldn't close them; I felt something strapped around my flesh, between my knees and my ankles. It hurt when I tried to move them in any direction.

'Dean, what are you doing?' I couldn't tell where he was. It was so dark.

'You'll see.' He was chuckling away to himself as though pleased with something he had done.

I tried to move the top half of my body, my hands were free and had not been tied but I couldn't move far. Why didn't I wake up before this? How the hell did a drunken maniac manage to tie me up while I was asleep? I guess it was true. I had always been told that a bomb could go off and I wouldn't wake up. I knew I was a heavy sleeper but this was ridiculous. I wanted to go back to my dream; I fared better with a shark than with Dean.

'Dean, where are you?' I asked into the darkness.

'I don't know.' He was still laughing to himself. 'Where are you?' He laughed harder now, pleased with the little joke he had made.

'Dean, untie me please,' I asked once more into the darkness, hoping he would listen and co-operate. I hoped he would be too drunk to do anything else.

'Ah. Not yet my pretty.' He was talking like the wicked witch who was after Dorothy in *The Wizard of Oz*, putting on a weird voice. 'Mmm. I'm going to have some fun with you first.'

'Dean, please let me get up. I can't move,' I begged him, wanting to cry.

'Oh, can't you? That's good because you move too

much anyway.' Suddenly he was lying flat on top of me. His naked body pressing hard against mine.

His wet lips pressed roughly against my cheek, pushing, searching, trying to turn my face so he could make contact with my mouth.

'No. No, Dean. Stop.' I struggled, pressing my face into the pillow. I could hardly breathe.

'If you don't stop moving then I'll have to tie your hands,' he slurred into my ear. Dean lifted himself up and was straddled across my hips. He lifted himself up some more and started rubbing his cock up and down the crevice in my backside, making himself hard.

By the time I realised what it was he was going to do there was nothing I could do but scream. He pushed himself forcefully into my back passage. I yelled loudly until one of his hands slammed down onto my open mouth. I bit his hand as hard as I could. I hoped it was the one he had hurt punching the wall earlier.

'You bitch.' He smashed his hand into the side of my face, the side that wasn't squashed against the pillow. He thrust harder, grunting loudly, increasing my pain. I had never felt anything like this before. It was bad; it hurt so much I couldn't stand it.

I tried scratching his legs with my fingers, each time I managed to dig into flesh he smacked me again. I could taste blood in my mouth.

Finally his torturous movements ceased and he rolled off me with a grunt. I lay spread-eagled on the bed. Numb.

Shocked. No longer aware of anything except the acidic blood flowing into my mouth.

I felt no pain.

'Ah. Gee, thanks, babe. That was fantastic.'

The jerk was sitting on the floor by the bed thanking me. I barely noticed his presence.

'Shit. Need a cigarette.' Dean got up and opened the bedroom door, walking out into the dimly lit hallway. He was back seconds later with smokes and lighter. He took one out of the packet and lit it, lying on the bed next to me. His legs draped heavily over my tied leg that was in his way.

I felt nothing.

He puffed away on his cigarette, whistling a tune I couldn't recognise and didn't care to try.

'Fuck. Forgot the ashtray,' Dean said, frustrated with himself for not remembering. Now he would have to get up again.

'Oh well. You'd make a good one,' he stated simply, probably wondering how he could have been so stupid not to have thought of that before.

So now he was ashing on me. Who cares? I was numb.

I felt nothing.

Dean continued to puff away and ash on my naked body.

I felt pain.

Searing pain.

I couldn't scream. The world went black.

I woke up feeling my legs being gently untied. My skin crawled beneath his touch.

'Leave me alone,' I said through swollen lips.

'Yeah. Hang on a second.' He sounded like he was doing me a favour. Like I should be grateful that he was helping me or something.

I didn't know what time it was; the sun was up and looked like it had been for some time. The room was brightly lit and I could hear sounds of life coming from outside.

'Where's Kate?' I tried hard to speak. I hurt everywhere and I didn't want to speak to him at all but I couldn't hear Kate and I wanted to know where she was. I needed to know.

'I've taken her to Mum's.'

Shit. How long had I been out?

'You don't want her to see you like this, do you?' he asked, as though I had done this to myself. How dare he. I wanted to smack him one. Real hard. Right in the face.

I'd only get away with it if I was strong enough to kill him. I hated him so much. I hated him more for untying me so bloody gently. I was in so much pain anyway from him. Why was he being so bloody careful? I wanted to scream at him, to throw myself at him and rip his eyes out. Would that kill him?

I didn't think it would and I didn't have the strength to try anyway. I wished he would hurry up and leave me alone.

Moments later my wish had been granted. Dean was gone. I stayed still on the bed, spread-eagled, just the way he had left me. I didn't even try to make a move until I heard the front gate creak as he pulled it closed.

As I tried to move the first painful inch, memories of the gruesome night came flooding back to me. Oh my God. What did he do to me? I was so sore.

I managed to get to the bathroom with a lot of limping and groaning. My legs were still quite numb. It was painful letting the blood rush back into them.

I noticed blood smeared all over the flower print sheet set my parents had given us last Christmas. The lower half of my legs, under my knees, had red welts raised in lines. My face felt swollen and I could still taste remnants of the blood that had flowed freely from my lip.

When I looked in the mirror I was shocked by what I saw. There was a fat-lipped, pummel-faced girl with dried blood in her hair staring at me. I didn't know who this stranger was at first. The girl with the sad face and pleading eyes.

I lowered my swollen head into my hands and turned to sit on the closed toilet lid.

I almost shot through the roof like a rocket when my skin made contact with the plastic seat. The pain was unbearable and I suddenly remembered being used as an ashtray.

I tried to turn and twist my aching body around to get a glimpse of my painful bottom. I ended up having to find a hand mirror in the vanity drawer.

I lifted the small mirror up to the area on my right butt cheek and saw two big round burns. Shit, I thought he only did it once. I slowly moved the little pink and white mirror to the left side, and saw three more of the fiery round burns. They were red in the middle and black on the outside. A blackened rim like a volcanic crater. There was still a cigarette embedded in one of the messy holes.

Dark, dried blood was smeared all over me, I couldn't tell exactly where it had come from.

I remember some things I prefer not to think about. But these are nothing compared to the things I can't think about – nasty, horrible, indescribable things. Things I cannot bear to bring near the surface. Things that would send me crazy if I allowed myself to think too much.

So I wiped them from my brain. No longer there. No longer able to reach the surface. I won't allow it. I can't allow it.

I ran myself a warm bath, which seemed pretty much useless because I couldn't sit down. I ended up standing naked in the tub full of water, washing myself with a facecloth.

I moaned as every part of me cried out for my hands to stop. I persevered, knowing the blood needed to be removed. I could then see more clearly the full extent of my injuries.

Ugly, bulging bruises were appearing on the pale skin of my back and thighs. There were no other burns apart from the five I had found earlier. I cried when the water hit these wounds. It hurt when I had to pull out the cigarette still lodged in my tender flesh.

Tears began to flow like rushing streams from my eyes. I didn't want to cry. I didn't want to be weak. I wanted to be strong. I stayed in the bathroom for some time, naked, standing in the cooling water, crying. Hating Dean and hating myself.

I emptied the pink-stained water and waited for the last of it to escape down the drain before grabbing the towel from the overhead rail and gently dabbing myself dry. Wincing at every light touch.

I emptied all the Band-Aids from the two boxes I found in the vanity along with an old squashed tube of antiseptic cream. I applied it liberally to the burns and dressed the wounds with all the Band-Aids except two. Once the raw open sores were covered to my satisfaction I looked at my face again in the small, wall-mounted mirror.

The only change from the last glimpse I had taken of this girl was that blood no longer clogged the strawberry-coloured hair. The face was still bruised and battered. The right eye had swollen up so much it was almost closed, the flesh an ugly mass of varying dark shades, from blue and purple to black. The cut on my lip was large and I taped it up with one of the Band-Aids I had kept for this purpose.

I thought of going to the doctor but knew I would be faced with a barrage of questions that I would not be able to answer. My last experience with the so-called justice system had left a lot to be desired. It was far too unpleasant a memory and I didn't want to repeat it. I couldn't cope with Dean being told he was right and I did not want to undergo another public humiliation. Once was enough, thank you very much.

I wished Kate were with me. I very much wanted to hold her in my arms. She would have made me feel better, she always did. I wondered whether Dean had gone to pick her up. I hoped so.

Dean didn't come back and neither did Kate. He didn't bring her back to me until three days later. All he said to me when he walked in the door with her following close behind was, 'Good, you don't look too bad now. Shouldn't give her any nightmares.'

I hugged her as tightly as my body would allow me to when she ran to me. I didn't want to let her go. Dean put her bags at the door and left again. I was grateful he wasn't sticking around. I wanted it to be just Kate and me. The misery that had engulfed me over the past few days quickly receded when I saw her little face smiling at me.

Joyful tears escaped my eyes; the swelling had mostly

gone now. I was surprised I could cry at all. I didn't think it would have been possible. I had cried an ocean thinking Dean had taken my baby girl and I would never see her again.

'Mummy sore.' Kate touched my face so lightly I barely felt it.

'It's okay, Katie. Mummy better now.' And it was true. It was all better now.

Chapter 6

I healed well but it was a slow process. My face and body took a couple of months before there was little sign of what had happened that night. The burns were taking longer and constantly bothered me. I had to get some thick gauze and tape to dress them properly but that did little to prevent them from becoming infected.

They were healing now but very, very slowly.

Kate was now two years and three weeks old. She had celebrated her second birthday in July. It was a quiet affair. My parents sent presents for her and she spoke to them on the phone. Dean brought his mother over for lunch, which lasted only an hour before he quickly ushered her out the door and drove her home.

Dean didn't come home very often any more. He would pop in to have a shower and change his clothes every couple of days. He would promptly vanish as quickly as he had come, without a word. I didn't know where he spent his time and I really didn't care.

I had started being sick again not long after the night Dean had damaged me. I couldn't keep anything down and was losing weight once more. It was the same feeling as before, which had been put down to stress. Yet it seemed to me that this time I was sicker.

I let it go on for four months before finally seeing the doctor. I was thin and pale, constantly exhausted. Dr Landers asked all the usual questions.

Was I eating properly? No.

Could I be allergic to anything? No.

Were my periods regular? No.

Could I be pregnant? What? No.

'No, no, I couldn't be. This is the same as last time and my period wasn't regular then either.'

I honestly hadn't considered pregnancy to be a possibility. I don't know why. It was highly probable. It had happened so many times before.

The thought bothered me. I didn't want to dispose of another human life, yet how could I bring it into this world?

I took myself to the little toilet cubicle at the end of the hallway for the urine sample that was needed to conduct the test. I was used to the routine and in less than five minutes I would know.

I wasn't shocked when the test returned a positive result. I wasn't shocked at all.

'C'mon, let's get you up on the table and see how far along you are. Then we can decide what to do.'

Dr Landers was a short, plump middle-aged man who wore large round glasses that looked too big for his face. He was a nice man and held me by the arm to help me onto the examination table. He was actually more of a hindrance than a help but it was a very nice gesture and I appreciated it.

He felt around my belly with his gentle, capable hands, pressing firmly as he went.

'It seems you may be at least sixteen weeks along, Amy.'

The doctor scratched his head as I sat up to swing my legs over the side of the table.

'Come, sit down.' He held my arm again and guided me to the brown padded chair located on one side of his shiny wooden desk. He positioned himself in the opposite chair, still obviously deep in contemplation.

'You are too far along for a termination this time, Amy,' he began. 'I can find you some help if you like,' he spoke fast, as though scared I would interrupt him. 'You don't have to live this way.'

'Thank you. I have tried help before.' It was all I could say. I stood up and left the room. Silently I plucked Kate from the playpen in the waiting area and walked home.

Kate wouldn't ride in a stroller at all any more. She had to walk everywhere, which could be extremely frustrating. Especially when I was in a hurry or just wanted to get home. She stopped to inspect anything unusual – and to her just about everything was unusual. She stopped to talk to ants and wanted to follow bees. She would stop to pick flowers and find pebbly treasures to fill up her pockets. It was hard to get her moving again when she found something she really liked and couldn't take it with her.

What was I going to do with another baby? The answer to that was I didn't know. I didn't know how to tell Dean. I didn't know if I should tell Dean. Although it wasn't as if I could keep it a secret for long – he was sure to figure it out at some stage. What was I going to do?

Dean waltzed into the house at about eight o'clock that night. I was watching television and Kate had been fast asleep for hours. I liked the nights. It was usually when I felt the best. The sickness escaped me for a few heavenly hours. It was at night that I tried to eat as much as I could. It was the only time I could keep any food down. It didn't bother me before whether I did keep it down or not but I had to now that I had another life to consider.

I was surprised when after his usual shower Dean sat on the couch opposite the one I was seated on and began watching the telly. He normally just had a shower and left. I was glad. I needed to talk to him. I didn't know if I wanted him to stay yet or not. That would depend on his reaction to my news.

We sat in silence, neither of us wanting to acknowledge the other person's presence. One hour went by, then two. I was having trouble building up the courage to say what I needed to.

'Dean,' I eventually said, testing the water to see how he reacted to me speaking at all.

'Yeah,' his gaze had not moved from the movie he was watching.

'We need to talk,' I continued cautiously.

'Do we?' he answered, still not looking at me. At least he had heard me. That was a good start and something I should be grateful for, I supposed. I really didn't know how I was going to proceed with this conversation. It had still not sunk into my own head.

'Um, Dean. I'm pregnant.' There you go, just blurt it out. I had no tact at all. That was something I probably needed to work on. I could have kicked myself. I'd blown any chance I had of breaking the news gently.

Dean's head slowly turned in my direction, his face lit only by the dim colours from the television.

'You're what? Shit, Amy. How could you do that?'

'So I did it on my own, did I? I am so clever.'

'How the fuck am I supposed to know who you're sleeping with?'

He wasn't yelling but he was angry. And so was I. How dare he accuse me of sleeping with anyone else.

'That's really low, Dean. When would I have the time? It's hard enough keeping up with you.'

My responses were now heavily laced with sarcasm. It was a talent I had picked up somewhere along the line and most of the time it got me into trouble.

'How do I know what you do when I'm not here?' He sat back in the couch with his arms folded across his chest.

'I'm looking after your daughter, that's what I'm doing.' All right, I was really angry now. I got up and stormed into the kitchen. I switched on the kettle and began making a cup of tea.

'Okay, settle down.' Dean was standing in the doorway of the kitchen. I swung around to face him.

'How dare you tell me to settle down, you bastard.' I was yelling at him. The fire in my belly had finally reached boiling point and was now overflowing. 'All you do is treat me like a piece of shit. You don't care about anything, do you, Dean?' I was letting him have it, and it felt good. 'You are a selfish prick and I hate you.'

I squeezed past him and ran to the bathroom, locking the door behind me. I sat on the cold tiles with my back against the door. I was so mad I was shaking. Tears threatened my eyes.

A few minutes later Dean was knocking on the door trying to catch my attention.

'Amy, come out and have a cone.'

He had cones. He didn't tell me that before. He'd been there for hours. Was he keeping it a secret on purpose? I had been worried about my smoking habits when I was pregnant with Kate. I told the doctors at the hospital when

I began attending my regular prenatal care appointments.

They were surprisingly more concerned with my smoking cigarettes than marijuana. Had they told me to give up I would have. If they had told me it would damage my baby then I would have stopped. But if they weren't concerned, why should I be? They were the doctors.

I got up and opened the door. Dean was in the lounge room when I came out. He had already mulled up and was packing the dope into the top of the hose attached to the imitation skull.

I sat down and smoked what was handed to me, holding the smoke inside my lungs for as long as I could, absorbing it into my body. Letting the feeling of relaxation wash over me. I was no longer angry. I could hardly remember what I had been angry about.

'So how far are you?' Dean thankfully had remembered the conversation.

'The doctor thinks about sixteen weeks,' I replied, sinking back into the soft, comfy couch. 'I only found out today.'

'How come you didn't know?' He was looking at me as if I must be stupid or something.

'My body is fucked up, Dean.' Now it was my turn to look at him as if he were stupid. 'Don't you get it? The things you do to me make me sick. I can't believe you don't get that.' I wanted to be angry. I wanted to be really angry, but I was too stoned to get mad.

Neither one of us spoke again that night. We remained

quiet. I was lost in my thoughts of how this baby was going to survive. I had enough trouble protecting Kate and myself from harm.

Dean was lost in his own thoughts. I don't know what they were. Maybe he wasn't thinking at all.

I went to bed and left him staring blindly into the television.

Dean remained home most of the time after our so-called discussion about the coming baby. My doctor called to make sure that I was all right and to tell me he had a referral organised for the prenatal clinic.

'It's imperative that you go straight away, Amy. You are already behind in your care.'

He was giving me the lecture my parents would have given me had they known what was happening. As yet I had not told them.

'Yes, I know. If I knew I was pregnant I would have seen someone,' I said in my defence. I must have sounded extremely irresponsible. Especially considering the fact that I had walked out of his office without waiting for the much-needed referral from him.

When I picked up the referral the next day I found that the good doctor had taken the liberty of making my first appointment. It was at two o'clock that afternoon. At least somebody cared, and this man was practically a stranger. Apart from the odd Pap smear test, he didn't know me very well at all. I was lucky to have such a caring doctor.

Dean looked after Kate while I took myself to the hospital for my first, very overdue appointment. It was horrible and took hours, worse than when I was pregnant with Kate.

It was a 'pick on Amy' opportunity. Dean should have come along; he would have been in his element, he could've joined in the fun.

'She's too skinny.'

'She's too pale.'

'Your blood pressure is a bit low. Has it always been like that?'

I was sent straight off for an ultrasound and to have blood taken. I felt like a piece of meat being poked and prodded, examined closely inside and out.

'What are all those lesions on you?' one of the nurses asked me as I was getting changed. She was very close and was touching my backside.

I had almost forgotten about the burns. Shit, what was I going to say?

'Oh, they're nothing.' I quickly straightened up, pulling my underwear up hurriedly to cover the offending area.

I continued to get dressed and the nurse left the room. Great. Well, this was going to be fun. Part of being a woman and the 'joy' of having a baby meant hanging around prenatal clinics with your pants off most of the time. I was going to have to answer each different person who was going to see me with my pants down. You never saw the same person twice in the hospital clinic. I was wishing I had the money to see a private gynaecologist.

At that moment I really wanted to give Dean a few scars of his own to explain. Imagine the humiliation.

'A woman did it, man. A crazy, crazy bitch.'

I laughed at the thought. In that context I didn't mind being thought of in such a way. I think he would rather die than admit to being hit by a girl. If I could do only half the things he had done to me I would be happy.

The blood tests proved I didn't have HIV or any other known diseases, which was always good to know, and the baby was doing fine. Surprisingly, as healthy as he or she should be.

The doctors were more amazed than I was. I think they were waiting for me to drop dead right in front of their eyes. As I was leaving the hospital I caught a glimpse of myself in the glass doors leading outside.

I saw what their faces had told. I had become one of the dead. The damned. My biggest fear was becoming a reality. It was hard to comprehend that the scrawny person reflected in the glass was me. I was part of the world of the living dead. I was one of them.

I had arranged to meet my parents for an afternoon by the river. They still did not know about the pregnancy. I had to tell them but needed to find the right time to do it.

I had to first get Dean's permission for the meeting. In the end he 'decided' it was the best thing. They had to know sometime.

I was five and a half months pregnant and still not showing so they would not yet know by looking at me, but I would not be able to hide it for much longer. I felt guilty for not telling them as soon as I had found out.

We met at a park along the Cox River, which marked the halfway point between our homes. It was a lovely park right on the river's edge. There was soft green grass, massive trees that gave shade in summer and there was lots of brightly-coloured play equipment. Kate was thrilled when she spotted the red, blue and yellow structures. There were swings, slippery slides and other fun things that would keep her amused. I knew I was never going to be able to get her off them when the time came to leave.

We sat at one of the many weathered wooden benches and tables. Mum had told me not to bring a thing. All we were to bring was ourselves.

Mum brought so much food with her it would have lasted me a week, at least. There was salad and cold roast chicken, cold beef, bread rolls, cake and fruit. I knew she would bring a lot. They always overdid it. They even brought a tablecloth to cover the picnic table.

'Are you having a glass of wine, Amy?' Mum always brought a bottle of wine to picnics.

'Ah. No thanks, Mum, I'll just have tea.'

I knew there would always be tea, coffee, hot chocolate and juice on these little outings.

They really were amazing. When I was growing up we went camping at least once a year. It was a blast. We took carpet for the tent and we had camp beds. There was no sleeping on the ground on our holidays. We camped in style. We even took our own toilet. True!

The tent was huge and took forever to assemble. It was like the Taj Mahal. Dad had to figure out where the sun would rise in the mornings. He liked the sun to come in and warm him up. Once we had put up the tent without checking the direction. The next day we all had to pull it down and turn it around in the pouring rain. After that incident we joked that we needed a tent on a lazy Susan so Dad could turn it around with the sun. Camping was a riot. We really knew how to get back to nature.

We had picked a table close to the playground for our picnic, knowing Kate would abandon us right away. We watched her play while we ate and talked. Kate had already eaten her lunch before we left home. Her eating times were dictated by her pre-programmed stomach: she ate at the same time each and every day.

I didn't know how I was going to tell them my news. It wasn't as though I thought they would be angry with me, just disappointed. I hated disappointing my parents. It was something I had become very good at. All I wanted was for them to be proud of me. But how could they, when I had done nothing to be proud of? My life was a mess and I didn't know how to clean it up. The worst part was that it was hurting not only me, but also all the people I loved.

Knowing there would never be a perfect time to tell them, I decided to just say it. After all, the situation would only be perfect if Dean was nice and I was happy. Like that was ever going to happen. I would just blend it in with the conversation.

'So, are you going to Dean's mother's for Christmas again this year?' We had gone to his mother's house every Christmas for the past three years.

'No, Mum. I'm coming to spend the day with you. I'm pregnant.'

Well, I'd said it. Maybe they hadn't noticed. Christmas was only five weeks away and I knew Mum was going to bring up the subject of who I would be spending it with. I missed my family Christmases. We had so much fun, opening masses of presents and consuming delicious food all day.

'Oh, Amy.' Mum looked at me, sadness clouding her blue eyes.

Dad didn't say anything. He just got up and went to push Kate on the swing. She was having trouble building up enough momentum to get moving. She didn't understand that she was too small to do it on her own. She didn't refuse Opa's help though, as I feared she would. She would never let me help her. She would just continue to sit there and get more and more frustrated with herself.

She sat up straight and smiled proudly as her Opa began to push her back and forth.

'You can't keep letting this happen.' Mum knew about the other pregnancies. I had told her about those. 'What are you going to do?'

'I am keeping this baby, Mum. I don't have any other choice this time.' I hoped she would understand without me having to explain much more because I didn't think I could.

The expression on her face told me she knew what I meant. She knew I had been sick again. I had kept in regular contact with her by phone. We even had our own secret code, just in case Dean was home. She would ring twice and hang up. I would ring her back. If she didn't get a call back she knew that Dean was there. Without Dean at home all the time I could talk to her whenever I wanted. Now he was there more often, it had become difficult again.

Mum walked around the table to where I sat and she hugged me. She cuddled me tightly; I breathed the smell of her familiar perfume. I think she was crying.

My next hospital appointment wasn't as long and torturous as the first one I had attended almost three weeks before. The doctor did a routine examination and a midwife completed current details, my blood pressure, temperature, weight, and so on. She was pleased to note

I had put on a kilo. This was thanks to my late-night binges. They were working. I was gaining weight.

Dean wouldn't look after Kate this time. I don't know why. All he said was, 'I've got something important to do.'

It was tiring having Kate there. While I was getting dressed and undressed she would start touching everything in sight. For this reason I was glad we didn't have to wait too long. It surprised me that we had only been there for an hour. It was the fastest appointment I had ever had. Even when I was pregnant with Kate they hadn't been this efficient.

I drove into our street and noticed a car in the driveway. A car I had never seen before. Dean must have made a new friend. I wondered where he'd met this one. Hopefully this guy would be decent, although Dean was not known to attract company from the civilised portion of the human race. He attracted the low-life population.

'Okay, Kate, let's go and meet this one,' I said, unstrapping her from the car seat.

'Look, my car, Mummy.' Kate was pointing at the faded red Toyota parked in my spot. Dean could have asked the guy to park on the nature strip, which was where I ended up.

I didn't know what Kate was talking about. Her car? It must have looked like one of her many toy cars. She liked Matchbox cars and managed to get a new one every time we went shopping. I had never known her to point one out before.

I opened the front door, letting Kate wander in under my outstretched arm. I expected to see Dean and his friend in the lounge room, but the couches were empty. The stereo was on and the only noise I could hear was INXS playing an early hit. I turned the television on so Kate could watch the cartoons, turning INXS off as she settled herself on the floor, already mesmerised by Bugs Bunny.

I opened the hallway door, which had been closed for some reason. It was normally only shut when Kate was sleeping. I heard Dean's voice coming from the bathroom: that door was also closed. I heard nothing else.

I walked up to the door and opened it. I don't know why. I had never opened a door without knocking first. Especially the bathroom door.

My toilet-cum-bathroom stool had now been turned into a love seat. Dean was sitting on it with his pants around his ankles and a head of long dark hair was in his lap.

'Oh, my God.' I had obviously said it loud enough for them to hear me. Startled, they stopped what they were doing and looked in my direction, obviously shocked by my unexpected presence. I too was shocked. The last thing I had expected when I walked in was the sight of Dean enjoying a head job in my bathroom.

I stood staring at them both. The image of what I had seen would not eject itself from my head. Everything else was a blur. The woman got up and pushed me out of the way, walking out while Dean finished doing up his jeans.

I heard a car start up outside and guessed it was the red Toyota belonging to the slut who had been in my house. I was standing in the hallway now after being shoved out of the way. I could feel anger beginning to build up right down in the pit of my stomach. Dean was still in the bathroom. He hadn't moved. I began to shake.

'I hate you,' I said, quite calmly.

Without another word I walked down the hall, past Kate who was still sitting on the floor watching cartoons and into the kitchen. I was making tea when I heard the front door slam and my car go racing up the road.

After he was gone I cried. He had probably gone to find his hussy. To comfort her about the misfortune of being found out. Never mind about me, the pregnant mother of his children.

Who was she? I had never seen her before. Then understanding hit me like someone had thrown a rock at my head. The car. The red Toyota that Kate seemed to know so well. That was where Dean had taken my daughter after his dark night of torture. He took her to stay at his whore's house, not his mother's. I had thought it odd that Sharon had never mentioned it and I didn't want to bring it up because I didn't know what Dean had told her was wrong with me. The thought of it all made my anger boil once more.

I had had a pretty good idea that Dean was sleeping around. I had suspected it for quite some time. He was not so demanding on me for sex, so I knew he must have been getting it from somewhere else. He couldn't cope without it. It wasn't this that made me so angry. It was the fact that he had done it in my home. This was my home! And he had taken Kate there, to her house. That was what made me the maddest. The maddest I had ever been.

I hated him. I really hated him.

Dean was back only an hour later. I was putting Kate to bed when I heard the car pull into the driveway. He had gone to score. After we were both stoned we talked. Dean's definition of talking, though, was different to mine.

'I can't believe you took Kate there. Wherever "there" is.' I said as calmly as I could.

'Well, she had to go somewhere.'

'Why, so she couldn't see how her father treats her mother?' Sarcasm was beginning to creep into my words. 'Don't you think she should see that, Dean?'

He said nothing. I didn't ask him who the other woman was. I didn't want to know; I really didn't care who she was.

'Don't ever take my daughter there again, Dean.' I was feeling courageous, but these feelings didn't last long; it took no time at all for Dean to knock them right back out of me.

He was bending over the top of me. I was pushed back into the couch, his finger pointing into my face.

'Don't demand anything of me, Amy. I own you and there will never be any escape. Don't underestimate me.'

Dean was spitting in my face as he spoke. He was so close to me.

'Leave me alone, Dean.' I was sick of taking his shit. I think being pregnant had made me a little more courageous than normal. I didn't dare speak up to him usually. I didn't think he would touch me while I was in this condition.

'You won't be pregnant forever, Amy. So watch what comes out of your mouth,' he replied, confirming my theory.

I despised him and wanted to tell him so. I didn't dare push my luck too far, though. I didn't yet want to see how far I could challenge him. I wasn't ready.

Kate and I had managed to spend Christmas Day with my family. It wasn't too hard to swing it. Now that I was starting to show a little, Dean didn't care too much what I did. If I repulsed him, then surely repulsion was the same reaction others would have towards me.

God, I repulsed myself. I had not put on any more weight and needed to attend fortnightly ultrasounds. The baby wasn't growing at the rate it should have been. It was not getting enough oxygen.

I was still sick, although in my previous experience that came with pregnancy. The morning sickness never goes away. It's a terrible feeling, like constant motion sickness. The problem was that I didn't know how much of it was due to morning sickness and how much to stress.

I worried about the baby. I told no-one about these concerns. Dean wouldn't have cared or would have found a way to blame me, so there was no point in telling him. I couldn't confide in my parents. I did not want to burden them with my problems once more. The only people who knew were the hospital staff and myself.

I had no-one's shoulder to cry on – I didn't have any friends left. There wasn't anyone. I had so many things to worry about; life was becoming a very heavy burden to bear.

When I was alone I would talk to my baby and beg it to live. Beg it to hold on. I was used to the idea now and I wanted to meet it. I had been told by the doctors to expect the worst. At each prenatal visit they were surprised that I hadn't miscarried yet. My appointments had been scheduled regularly, twice as often as the women with 'normal' pregnancies.

Kate was well known throughout the hospital and had everyone wrapped around her little finger. She did that to people.

The doctors told me to go home and rest, which was something I had forgotten how to do. I had forgotten how to live without feeling on edge. There didn't seem to be a time when I wasn't feeling anxious. My household was a very stressful place to be. It really was normal to expect the unexpected. To always expect the worst that any given situation could present. Being bashed up a bit seemed better than some of the other possibilities I could imagine.

You go past feeling scared. I used to feel scared all the time. That feeling mutates into something worse. It's like a never-ending internal pain. Nothing makes it go away. It was like there was a part of me missing. It is hard to put my finger on, but it was an odd feeling.

Maybe Dean had messed me up some more after knocking me unconscious. Or maybe it was a side effect of being beaten senseless so many times. But something was definitely missing.

I found it for a little while on Christmas Day. My family always made me feel loved, special, beautiful and worthwhile. Nothing was too much trouble for them. Their love was unconditional. It was their love that was special, not me.

My parents had gone all out. They had bought so many presents it was shameful. They had always overdone the presents, even when we were kids. We got a lot more than our friends did and I won't say it didn't feel good, because it did. When you're a kid it matters. They had set an impossible precedent, however; how was I going to match it? They outdid themselves every year and this year was no exception.

I felt guilty for not being able to give Kate all the things I had been blessed with when growing up.

Kate's day was made from the moment we arrived. There was a pink tricycle with a big blue ribbon tied around it sitting on the front lawn. She screeched and squealed so loudly it was deafening, but she wasn't stopping there. She wanted to see what else there was. Even a two-year-old knew to expect more at Oma and Opa's.

She didn't even stop to touch the little trike. My only thought was that she may only be two years old, but her behaviour was just plain rude. I barged inside after her to let her know, in her language, just what I thought.

There was no getting near her. She was surrounded. Grandparents, aunties and presents. Kate was gone, swallowed up in a sea of adoring admirers bearing gifts. Not a bad position to be in, really.

It was a hot day. Mum and Dad lived quite high up in the mountains so it wasn't as hot as it was down on the plain. It was scorching where I lived.

Mum had different platters set out on the large dining room table. There were prawns, salad, cold pork and chicken. Fruit, cheese and crackers, chocolate and mince pies.

The table was crammed with food all day. When you felt hungry you ate. We had never had a hot Christmas dinner. My mother was always too busy enjoying herself to be cooped up in a hot kitchen, and I agreed with this. The first time I had had a hot meal at Christmas was with Dean's family.

The women had come out of the kitchen proudly showing off the beautiful roast pork, chicken and baked vegetables. The only problem was that they looked like they were ready to pass out. Their faces were red and sweat was trickling down their foreheads. I could not think of a worse way to celebrate a special occasion. I was with my mother on this one. Cold food and paper plates. No mess, no fuss.

We all behaved like complete fruit loops. Our heads were adorned with headbands complete with flashing lights. Carols played in the background. There was dancing and lots of laughter. I was having so much fun.

By mid-afternoon I was exhausted. I sat in one of the padded outdoor chairs under the back verandah. My sisters were having a water fight with Kate, Mum also joining in the fun.

I sat back and watched them play. Dad sat next to me drinking a cool shandy. My dad is a man of few words. I think it came from living with so many women for so long. When we all started suffering from PMS, I am sure it must have been unbearable for him. There were many times I remember when he only had to say 'Good morning' to one of us and we would run off in tears. The poor man. He only spoke when he had something important to say. It was normal to sit for hours in the same room with him in total silence. It was a comfortable silence.

Kate was saturated and tired from her afternoon of fun-filled water games. By four o'clock she had been changed into a dry outfit Mum had given her. It was a red sundress with a Christmas print. She had fallen asleep on my sister's bed cuddling an old teddy bear.

I was contemplating staying the night. I was far too tired to drive home and I was starting to feel off-colour again.

I found Mum in the living room packing all of Kate's new toys into giant Santa sacks, purchased just for this reason, I was sure. There was so much of it. New clothes, Barbie dolls and accessories and a baby doll that ate and needed her nappies to be changed. There was the trike and colouring-in books. It was an amazing sight.

'Is it all right if Kate and I sleep over, Mum?'

'Of course you can, Amy. You don't need to ask.' Mum was looking up at me from her crouched position on the floor, a look of concern covering her pretty face. People had always commented on her looks. From the time I first started school people had always told me how pretty my mother was. She stood up and came over to me, putting her arm lovingly around my shoulders. She guided me to one of the reclining armchairs and turned me around, sitting me down as you would a naughty child.

'You sit there and don't move,' she was pointing her finger at me. 'I'll go and get the phone and you can give Dean a call to let him know. Do you think he will mind?'

'You know, Mum? I really don't care,' I replied, not convincing myself. He would care but I wanted to delay going back as long as I could. Now that I was here I didn't want to leave.

Mum came back with the cordless phone and I dialled my home number. There was no answer. I dialled Dean's mother's number, thinking he would still be there if he wasn't at home.

'Hi Sharon, Merry Christmas,' I said in reply to her cheery greeting. 'Is Dean there?'

'No, he went home hours ago. Have you tried your house?'

I told her that I had, but she had no idea where he could be. I guessed he was with the red Datsun. I put the phone down and decided to try again later.

But I never did. I was so exhausted I fell asleep and didn't wake up until the next morning. To make matters worse Mum and Dad had let me sleep in, amusing Kate out in the garden. They were only trying to help and didn't know that they had done the opposite. I didn't say anything to them.

It was after eleven when I drove into my driveway. It had taken ages to fit all the extra goods into the car and say our goodbyes. It was always hard for me to say goodbye to my family.

I closed the gates behind the car and opened the boot. I removed the pink tricycle and gave it to Kate who was standing beside me waiting eagerly to ride it. I was glad because I didn't want her coming into the house right away. I wanted to see how I was greeted alone first.

'Here you go.' I watched her climb onto the seat and said to her, 'Katie, you stay here and ride your new bike. Mummy will be out soon. Okay?' I waited for her to nod her head to acknowledge that she had heard my instructions.

I walked up the steps to the front door leaving Kate happily riding around in circles on the concrete. When I opened the door Dean was standing at the far end of the room with his arms folded across his broad chest.

'Where have you been?' he demanded in a low growl.

'I was too tired to drive so I stayed at Mum and Dad's,' I replied. 'I tried to call you but you weren't here.'

I walked into the hall and made my way to the bedroom with the bag I carried. Dean was close behind me.

'Don't you fucking walk away from me.' It was the same deep growl.

I kept walking.

Dean grabbed hold of my arm and twirled me around in a rough pirouette to face him.

'I said don't fuckin' walk away from me.'

'Why do you care, Dean?' I asked. 'Why do you care what I do when you hate me so much?'

I felt my back slam hard against the wall in reply. His hands were wrapped tightly around the tops of my arms. I was winded and couldn't breathe. I was in shock; his movements had been quick.

'See, you don't even care that I'm pregnant,' I managed to say.

'You're right. I don't give a fuck,' he was yelling at me, 'it's probably not my kid anyway.' Okay, we had been through this before. 'All you are is a fucking slut.'

Dean let go of one of my arms, tightening his grip on the other one to prevent me from moving far. I heard the zipper in his pants come down.

'Get on your knees,' he demanded.

'No.'

'I – said – get – on – your – knees.' He emphasised each word while he firmly pushed me down. I tried to resist but he was too strong. He had a fistful of my hair, squeezing close to the scalp for greater control. I was now in a crouching position, my face in front of his crotch.

He forced his erect penis into my mouth, pushing hard into the back of my throat. I made a choking sound, retching. He moved himself back to plunge inside again. I bit him, hard, my teeth firmly embedding themselves in the hardened flesh. I heard Dean yell out painfully and felt a massive blow at the side of my head, close to my eye. I was thrown sideways, landing hard on the mottled-blue carpeted floor.

Dean launched over me, grabbing my hair again, and dragged me into the lounge room.

'Why do you make me do this?' He was yelling at me, dragging me across the carpet. 'Why can't you just shut up?'

'Dean, stop.' I screamed back at him, my head and body burning. 'The baby.'

'The fucking baby? I told you I don't give a shit about the damn baby.'

The tension on my head lessened as he let go of my tangled hair. He bent down, fire raging in his eyes. He lifted my dress up and held the growing mound that housed our unborn child. He gripped my belly hard, hands open, palms flat, fingers outstretched. Pushing down, twisting.

'Dean, stop. Please stop.' I was screaming at him, struggling. Trying to push his strong hands away.

'I hate this baby.' He growled through clenched teeth. 'I hate it and I hate you.'

He squeezed once more, harder this time, as if trying to strangle the baby from the outside. He got up and spat in my face, saliva running into my ear. With that he stormed out of the house.

I wiped his filth from my face with the hem of the dress that was resting at my neck after Dean had exposed me. I lowered the blue cotton dress back down and lifted myself into a sitting position.

Kate was standing next to the couch. How long had she been there? What did she see? She walked over to me and put her arms around my neck. Patting me with her little hands she said, 'It's okay, Mummy.'

It was my job, a mother's job, to comfort my child. Yet, in her short life, Kate had so far been the one doing the comforting. She never cried. When I was sitting with my head in the toilet bowl, as I often did, throwing up, Kate stood by me and would rub my back gently. It was Kate who would get the wet facecloth and wipe my face down. She was only a toddler and she was doing the looking after.

I sat her in my lap, her arms still locked firmly around my neck. Tears fell silently down my face. Tears for Katie. Tears for the baby. Tears for me. I held back the loud sobs trying to escape. I didn't want to be sad.

I wanted to be angry. I should be angry.

'Stop taking this shit, Amy,' I said to myself. 'Get up and fight.' Fiona's words came back to me. The words she had said to me.

'No-one will help you, Amy. You have to do whatever it takes. Learn to beat him at his own game.' It felt like an eternity ago.

'I've had enough, Katie,' I said into my daughter's hair, barely audible. 'It's time to fight. I'd rather die trying than not try at all.'

As if in response to what I had said there was a strong movement in my belly. I held my breath. It was the first time the baby had moved. I should have been worried after all that had just happened, but I wasn't. I smiled and tightened my hold on Katie.

I knew what I had to do. I needed a plan.

'C'mon, Katie, we're going for a drive.'

I went to the bathroom to have a look at the damage. My eye was cut and blood had trickled down my face. I didn't bother washing it away. I had carpet burn on my legs, a lump on my head and faint bruises were beginning to appear on my belly and arms. I knew they would be black tomorrow.

Chapter 7

My plan was simple. If the police and the so-called 'justice system' failed to help, then I would kill Dean and if I was unsuccessful I would bide my time and find the people to help me. That would be my last resort – these were people I only wanted to get tangled up with if I had no other choice.

I had worked out a three-step program. Three easy steps and you're free. It sounded like a quit smoking advertising campaign. Nevertheless, it was my plan and it was all I had.

Phase one was not proving effective. I had already decided in only three weeks that I hated the police. They were no help. They were arseholes.

I had thought my first impression of them might have been wrong, but no, first impressions count. It was now official – they were unsympathetic shits.

After the Boxing Day incident I drove to the police station with Kate. The dried blood trail from my cut eye was still plainly visible. I looked like a complete wreck and obviously pregnant. I walked into the station, half-dragging Kate behind me.

The guy at the counter in his smart police uniform looked at me and said, 'Are you all right, miss?'

Was he blind?

'Do I look all right?' was my reply.

'Huh,' he actually chuckled. Did he think I was joking? He really was an idiot.

'Is there anyone here in charge?' I asked, hoping he wasn't going to tell me it was him. I think I would have turned and run.

'Okay. Calm down. I'll go get the sarge.' He looked at me strangely then sauntered off through an open doorway that looked like it led down a long corridor.

He came back five minutes later with a short, fat, balding man in uniform.

'I'm Sergeant Thompson. How can I help you?' he introduced himself from behind the counter. Was he blind too? How can I help you? Wasn't it obvious?

'Well, I hope you can,' I began, more than a little bewildered. 'My boyfriend keeps bashing me up and I need you to help me. I'm pregnant and he won't stop.' I was practically begging, the words coming out in a rush.

'So apply for a restraining order,' he said simply, adding, 'you do know what that is, don't you?'

'Yes, I know what that is. I've tried and they wouldn't give me one.'

'Well, why do you think that might be?' he asked, leaning over the bench, taking everything in with a giant smirk covering his face. Probably thinking this was going to be a good story to have a laugh with the boys about later.

'Because Dean is a liar. He said I was crazy and they believed him.'

'Mmm, thought there must have been something. Magistrates usually give those things out like water.' Now he was insinuating that I was crazy.

'Do you think this is funny?' I asked. I couldn't contain myself any longer. 'Look at me.'

'Yeah, I'm looking. But if the magistrate wouldn't help you, then what do you want me to do?'

Oh my God. This was so frustrating.

'Don't you understand that I am scared? I need protection. I need you to take us somewhere so he can't find us.' I was pleading, tears forming behind my eyes. The balding police sergeant leaned further over the counter and looked down at Kate. I think he had only just noticed her presence.

'That his child?' he asked.

'Yes, she is.'

'Well, he has to know where she is. Even if you left him he would have to know where you live. He's her father. It's his right,' he explained. He pulled a lollypop from a glass jar on one of the desks and came around the counter, handing the lolly to Kate. Maybe he wasn't so bad after all.

'Please,' I turned to him. 'You have to help us.'

'Do you need hospital treatment?' he asked. I was puzzled.

'No.'

'And you're not dead,' he stated, looking at me.

'Not yet.'

'Then because you're not in hospital or dead, there is nothing we can do.'

I was shocked. I couldn't believe he had said that. I had to be dead to get help? What was the point in that? I sank slowly to the ground. Kate was still beside me sucking the green lollypop the sergeant had given her. My eyes were moist. All I ever did any more was cry, and I cried now. I looked up at the man in uniform before me, feeling like a lost child. I clasped my hands together as if in prayer, kneeling on the grey-carpeted foyer of the police station.

'Please. Please help me,' I begged.

The fat man spun on his heel and slunk back to where he had come from. Ignoring my pathetic pleas.

So phase one had failed miserably. Whenever I'd had anything to do with the system I had been left humiliated and even more defeated than I'd felt before the encounter.

It was now time to work on phase two. Killing Dean.

My belly was slowly growing, which meant my baby was growing larger. I still had the regular ultrasound check-ups. It was a virtually impossible task trying to hide the bruising black fingermarks adorning my milky-white flesh.The same people had noticed the burns and the only thing I could do was dodge their questions by changing the subject.

I decided, when the New Year arrived, that I was going to take some control back from Dean. I still didn't know how, but I would find a way. I thought about ways to kill him all the time. I would cook up devious little schemes in my head. Sometimes I would look at Dean and smile. Sometimes he would smile back.

Little did he know that I was seeing his handsome head roll right off his shoulders. It was kind of fun thinking up different ways to bump him off. I'm not ashamed to say it kept me going. Let's just say it gave me a goal, something to strive for, something to achieve. It was a lot less depressing to think about his death than to think of my own. Before, the only thoughts travelling around my mind were of ways he was going to use to kill me. Now I was having much more fun.

I thought of poisoning his food, stabbing him while he slept and running him over a hundred times with the car. There were so many things I could do I had trouble trying to decide on one. It's sick, I know, but these crazy thoughts empowered me somehow. Everything was not lost yet.

On my twenty-first birthday Sharon looked after Kate, and Dean took me out for dinner. It was only the second time he had ever done it and I don't know why he did. I was pregnant on both my eighteenth and twenty-first birthdays. I felt ripped off and gloomy and just wanted to stay home. I especially didn't want to go out with a man I hated. I was seven and a half months pregnant and wasn't in the mood for a pretend happy families moment.

The Lonestar Restaurant was filled with noisy people and as Dean had neglected to book a table we had to wait for one to be vacated. It was a horrible night. Dean worked his public personality like a charm. His killer smile was more deadly than they all realised.

If pregnancy and stress had not already made me nauseous, Dean's performances never failed to create that unpleasant sensation. It was draining putting on such a convincing act. I didn't know how he kept up the charade. I was exhausted enough just watching him.

I tried to be nice back to him but I just couldn't.

Thankfully, it wasn't a late night. I knew my attitude had contributed to this fact and that it had pissed Dean off, but quite frankly I couldn't give two hoots.

'Jesus, I can't even try to do anything nice for you, can I? There's never any thanks. You just behave like a complete bitch,' Dean had said to me in the car on the drive home. He was picking up Kate in the morning.

He was unbelievable. After everything he had done he

expected me to thank him for taking me to dinner. On my birthday! I didn't answer him. I didn't speak to him at all. I just went straight to bed.

On my last ultrasound appointment I asked about the sex of the baby.

'You already have a little girl, don't you?' the technician asked.

'Yes,' I nodded.

'Well that's good because you're not getting another one.' He said this with a smile on his face. I think he liked giving people this news.

I lay in bed hearing Dean tinkering in the kitchen. I stroked my belly, trying to picture what my son would look like. I wouldn't see him for another couple of months yet and I was getting impatient already.

When I had left Dean when Kate was a baby I had stayed on the pension. I had neglected to tell Social Security that we were living together again for the simple reason that this meant I had money that Dean could not get to. This gave me the opportunity to purchase a few things for the baby, something I had not been able to do when pregnant with Kate. It also meant keeping her decently clad and keeping us from starving. I enjoyed buying the tiny blue outfits. I always hid them in Kate's cupboard to keep them away from Dean.

I had started seeing Fiona again. When Dean went out I was able to race around to her place for a visit.

Sometimes she would see his car drive past as he left and would come over and have a cuppa with me. Even though I had become very friendly with her again, and she was the only friend I had, I didn't tell her everything. I didn't feel the need to. I had once, but not now. Whingeing to other people wasn't going to get me out of my situation. I liked talking to Fiona to get away from it. We mostly talked about kids. Neither one of us did anything else but raise children, so there was really nothing else to talk about.

With seven kids in the house, Fiona had a multitude of funny stories to tell. Children were so inventive. It was hysterical.

'You know,' she was laughing as she spoke. 'I have absolutely no idea what I am doing. I just tell myself I have control over them, when really they're the ones who control me. No wonder I am always constipated. They don't even let me go to the loo without seven pairs of hands trying to break down the door.'

We were laughing so hard I almost wet my pants. She was so much fun to talk to. I didn't laugh nearly enough.

If we were at Fiona's house we would sit at the dining room table so we could see out the front door. This way we could see the cars passing on the road. If we saw Dean return home before me, Fiona would plant a good-sized bud of marijuana into my palm.

'It's on me. Tell him I gave it to you on credit.'

She always wished me luck before ushering me out the

door. Whenever this happened and I returned with the smoko there wasn't usually a problem. If Dean got something out of it then it was all right.

I started learning to think about everything I did. Learning to do things in a way that benefited Dean. It only had to be in a small way and it worked most of the time. I was learning what worked and what didn't. If I didn't get hit, it had worked. I began to know how a boxer felt. The more you get pummelled, the more you want to prove how much you can stand up to it. You get a rush from the strength you have gained by standing up and not buckling under the pressure. That feeling was exhilarating. It made the pain mutate into something else.

The more I showed that what he did to me didn't hurt, the more frustrated Dean became.

My feelings of hatred towards Dean continued to grow with each passing day. I preferred to stay lost in my thoughts and pretend he wasn't there. I tried to ignore his insults and vicious taunts. The times I had trouble biting my tongue, unable to resist the urge for retaliation, still came often, and I always paid the price.

It had been a terrible day. I was now heavily pregnant. I had a big round tummy while the rest of me was bone. I was a stick figure with a protruding waistline.

Dean had not stopped from the moment he got out of

bed. It was the usual stuff: 'You can't do anything right.' 'You're a worthless bitch.' 'I hope you die giving birth to that kid.' And so on.

After I had put Kate to bed that night I went to the kitchen to finish the cleaning up from dinner. I was thinking of different things, mostly Dean's harsh words. The words he had spoken over the past 24 hours had dug deep. I began to feel anger rise, bubbling like lava from an erupting volcano.

I walked into the living room to get a dirty mug from the coffee table. Dean had fallen asleep on the couch, his head resting on its cushioned arm.

I walked past, shooting him a look that reflected my feelings for him. I put the mug in the sink and picked up the heavy cast-iron frypan to put it away in the cupboard under the sink.

I felt its weight in my hand and wondered suddenly if it would be heavy enough to kill him.

Without another thought I carried the pan back into the other room. The only sounds came from the radio in the background; I will never forget the song that was playing at the time. Aretha Franklin was belting out the words to 'Respect'.

I stood over Dean's sleeping head, hatred filling every pore, overwhelming me. Aretha continued singing the words – 'R-E-S-P-E-C-T/Find out what it means to me' – and I lifted the heavy pan, both hands gripping the handle tightly. As I lowered the pan I had second thoughts – what if it didn't kill him? I hesitated, but the momentum had begun and it was too late to stop it. The pan fell, smashing onto Dean's snoring face. I felt myself go numb, like the blood had suddenly drained out of me. I knew it hadn't killed him, my moment of hesitation prevented the bone-shattering force I was hoping for. At the very least though, it should have knocked him out. I was surprised that it hadn't.

His nose had been completely flattened, obviously broken, and there was blood everywhere. He was almost screaming with the pain, trying to wipe the blood from his eyes, not knowing what had brought him out of his peaceful dreamy state. All he would have felt was the tremendous terror of not knowing what was happening. At least he now knew how that felt. How I felt each time it was done to me.

I was frozen, my legs unable to move. I had no feeling anywhere in my body. I just stood there staring in shock at the blood-stained monster writhing on the couch below me. I felt nothing and thought nothing.

It was stupid of me. I should have been running. It wouldn't have taken him long to outrun me in my condition but I should have been trying. It would have been better than what was to come.

I came to life the moment I realised Dean was no longer lying down. He was standing up, and he was really pissed off. I made a move towards the door but Dean was faster. You would not have thought he had just had his face smashed in with the huge cast-iron pan, which was now lying discarded on the floor.

The only evidence was the damaged face staring at me with deadly intent. Before I had reached the door Dean had me. He held me roughly and slapped my face. It was so hard I thought my head was going to be ripped from my shoulders. He picked me up and took a step through the door into the warm March evening.

Suddenly I was flying through the air, landing with a painful thud at the bottom of the steps. I had landed only centimetres from the concrete path that led to the gate.

Without a word from Dean the front door slammed shut and I heard the dead bolt lock into place.

Shit, he had locked me out. Kate was still inside and I had been thrown out like a piece of garbage. I felt a sharp pain creep over my abdomen.

'Oh my God,' I moaned, gripping my large tummy. 'Not now, baby. Not yet, please not yet.'

I was still lying on the patchy grass. I felt something moist between my legs and reached down with my hand to see what it was. I lifted my hand back up to my eyes and felt sick when I saw the dark red substance covering my fingers.

There was another pain as I tried to get up, another pain from the baby. I didn't think I had any broken bones. I probably would have if I had landed on the concrete. My primary concerns – at this moment, anyway – were the baby I still carried and the one that had been left inside the house. As if sensing my fears I heard Kate start crying.

The sound came from her bedroom. Kate's room was the last window that faced the verandah I was now sitting at the bottom of, bleeding and sore. I heard her cries get louder and wondered if Dean had heard her.

'Will you shut the fuck up!' His violent yells answered my question and I heard a door slam. Kate's cries became louder and more hysterical.

'Mummy, Mummy,' she cried over and over again. 'I want my Mummy.'

I pushed myself up painfully, until I was standing. I climbed back up the stairs and knocked loudly on the door.

'Dean, let me in,' I yelled, hoping he would hear me. 'Dean let me in, I'm bleeding.'

'You're not coming in so fuck off,' he screamed back at me, through the door.

I turned and started making my way back down the steps. There was no point standing up there arguing with him, I needed help. Another sharp pain took over when I was halfway down. I gasped, trying not to fall over. I closed my eyes and waited until the pain subsided. Eventually I made my way to Fiona's house.

Fiona was waiting for me inside her door. She had seen me coming down the road but was unable to come outside to help me. I didn't blame her for that. It was just the way things were. People don't get involved. It could mean big trouble for them if they did. Fiona was taking a big enough risk just letting me into her home.

'Can I use your phone?' I asked. I was trying to stay as focused as I could, stamp out the panic building inside me.

Fiona helped me to the phone, offering to make the calls for me. I declined her offer, needing to do this for myself. I dialled 000 and Fiona went to get me a towel to clean myself up.

I was so worried about my baby. I was also worried about Kate. I feared what Dean could do to her if she continued to cry the way she was. It made my heart ache.

The emergency operator on the phone instructed me that the police and ambulance had been notified and were on their way. I hung up the phone and looked at Fiona.

'I have to get back there,' I said to her, heading back to the door.

'Wait, Amy.' Fiona caught me gently by the arm.

I felt another wave of pain tighten my belly. I held my breath, holding tightly onto Fiona, waiting for it to pass.

'I have to see if she's all right.' I was breathing again. The pain had gone and I was on the verge of tears.

'I'm sure Kate will be fine. Think about the baby for now, Amy. Concentrate on that.' I knew she was only trying to help. She was speaking softly, trying to keep me calm.

On one hand what Fiona was saying was right, I did need to concentrate on my son. He wasn't due to leave his snug home for another three and a half weeks. On the other hand, though, I knew what Dean was capable of; I feared what he might do to Kate.

God, I couldn't think straight. I was confused and didn't know what to do. Suddenly we heard sirens screaming closer. As the noise grew louder we saw the blue and red flashing lights as they approached. There were two police paddy wagons and two ambulances. I met them outside and two of the police officers took me into the back of an ambulance to join the paramedics.

All the necessary questioning began and relevant details were written down. The paramedic turned to one of the officers and said, 'Sorry, mate. You'll have to do this later. We've gotta get her to a hospital.'

The young policeman didn't look impressed. And neither did I.

Dean wasn't co-operating; the other two policemen had established this. They had knocked on the door and were met with vicious threats from inside the house. He was not letting Kate out. This he had made clear. Even from the back of the ambulance I could still hear her cries.

'Okay, you take her. We'll sort this out and get the rest of her statement later.' They were discussing me as if I wasn't even there.

'I'm not going anywhere without my daughter,' I said more forcefully than I thought I was capable of. Then I started to cry.

The policeman bent over me, a hint of sympathy in his kind green eyes.

'I promise I will get your daughter out and I promise that I will personally bring her to you. Okay?'

Sobbing through the pain of another contraction, I let them take me away. I had left Kate behind, calling for me. I had let her down and I knew it was all my fault.

By the time the ambulance arrived at the hospital my waters had broken and the contractions were bearing down on me, thick and fast. There were no painkillers this time; the contractions were too close together. This was going to be a quick labour.

'I have to push,' I screamed as they wheeled me through the open double glass doors.

'Hold on, we're nearly there. Breathe,' the doctor walking beside the trolley said to me.

As I was panting, the doctor and the paramedics discussed how many centimetres I had dilated and other vital statistics.

'I really have to push,' I screamed again as they wheeled me into the birthing suite. I tried to pant to prevent the overpowering urges.

As soon as they wheeled me in place I was hoisted by the sheet underneath me onto the bed parallel to me, which had been readied for this event.

'Okay, Amy, here we go.' The young doctor was at my feet. An Asian man with large almond eyes, he was very kind and his touch was gentle. I was glad it was him. I had seen Dr Hung on a couple of the prenatal visits and had liked him from the start.

'All right, Amy. On the next contraction I want you to push.' Dr Hung spoke in a voice that was soft and calming. He spoke slowly, looking right in my eyes, making sure I had heard his instructions. He was worried, I could tell. He had always been worried about my baby and me and had let me know this before.

I was sweating, my face damp, my mouth dry. On the next contraction I pushed, bearing down as hard as I could. Only minutes later my son was born. The room was silent. There were no loud baby cries as there had been when Kate was born. There was nothing. I didn't even get a glimpse of him before they rushed him away to another room.

I could hear them working. I didn't know what was happening. I was stricken with fear: I didn't know if my baby was alive or dead.

The doctor came back and sat on a chair beside the bed.

'Your baby is going to be fine, I think,' he began. 'He wasn't breathing, but he is now. We are just checking him over properly and giving him a wash and we will bring him right back to you. Okay?'

I nodded, tears rolling down my face. It had been two hours since Dean had thrown me out the door.

The doctor asked if there was anybody he could call for me. I told him that I needed to speak to my mother. I still had heard nothing about Kate. He went to arrange for a phone to be brought to my room.

While the doctor was gone a midwife brought my tiny son in to me. She placed the feather-light bundle in my arms. He was so small; there was nothing of him. He didn't look like Kate had when she was born. She had been chubbier.

This tiny boy looked like a miniature person. All of his features stood out. Not squashed like most babies.

'He gave us a bit of a fright. He's fine though, strong for such a little fella, and after everything you've both been through.' The midwife shook her head as she wheeled the clear plastic crib closer to the bed. She told me that he only weighed just on 5 pounds.

Wrapped snugly in the blue baby blanket, he looked up at me, his eyes opened wide. He was gorgeous.

When Dr Hung returned with the phone I called Mum. I needed her to find out where Kate was because I had no idea what was going on. The baby and I were left alone in the large white room to allow me to speak privately.

As Mum answered the phone the hospital room door opened and the policeman from the ambulance came walking in, with Kate sitting high up in his arms wearing his police hat.

'Mummy,' she called.

I told Mum that she had a grandson and asked if she could come to the hospital. The rest didn't matter any more. I had my Kate and my baby boy. Nothing else in the world mattered.

I cuddled my babies close, kissing both their heads. I vowed never to leave them and that I would do everything in my power to protect them. I would never risk their lives again. I had been stupid. My heart had split in two and had transformed into these little angels. My heart now walked with them. I had to protect my heart.

Mum arrived an hour and a half later, a smile stretching from ear to ear. As always she brought gifts – obviously she had stopped at the gift shop on her way up to the maternity ward. We had been moved to maternity not long after my happy reunion with Kate, who had been thrilled with her baby brother and smothered his tiny face with kisses.

I gave my statement to Constable King, who turned out to be a very nice cop after all. Maybe they weren't all so bad. Maybe it's only some of them who go on a power trip when in uniform. I wished there were more like Constable King. I hoped he wasn't as rare as I feared his type might be.

The constable sat down and explained everything that had happened before his arrival at the hospital. He told me that they had ended up sending dogs in the house to get Dean. They had decided to do this because Kate was shut in her room. A policewoman had talked to her at her window but Kate was too small to lift the heavy windows to get out so they felt they had no other choice.

The dogs had been sent in and attacked Dean after he had thrown one of the policemen over his shoulder. Dean was now at another hospital being stitched up from the numerous bites, and having his broken nose taped up as a result of my frypan and me.

Constable King had assured me that with what he had seen, a restraining order would now be granted. His own evidence would be enough to justify the need.

Mum took Kate back home with her, and would keep her at her place until I was out of hospital.

I spent the remainder of the night staring lovingly into the face of my sleeping son. He would be called Jack.

My parents had decided to move the children and me out of Clairvale and into a house closer to them. I was grateful for this, as I didn't want to take the kids back to the colourless suburb of the damned.

Three weeks later Kate, little Jack and I were living in a small three-bedroom cottage in the mountains. I had had to attend court to obtain the restraining order. It was easy this time, and Dean had not appeared to contest it.

I had heard nothing from him. I had most of the furniture from the Clairvale house – a few things had been left for Dean, but I had taken most of it, and my car. My children were safe and Dean wasn't allowed near me for the next twelve months. All was good. Jack was putting on weight. The doctors were amazed at how healthy he was after such an eventful pregnancy and premature birth. He slept a lot, only waking when he was hungry. He had a very small cry and there were times when I didn't hear him straight away.

Katie loved helping me look after her baby brother.

She would get nappies from Jack's room when the time came to change him and she helped bathe and feed him. If the pacifier fell out of his mouth and he whimpered, Kate would run over and put it back in for him, waiting to make sure he started sucking on it again and went back to sleep. She loved her baby brother very much.

Jack had a very different temperament to Kate. He didn't cry the way she had at his age. Jack was sleeping through the night at eight weeks old. Kate was almost three and had only just started to sleep through the night now. But the more weight little Jack put on the more he began to look like his sister. I didn't think he would ever get to be as chubby as Kate had been, though. He was so much smaller.

At first the smallest size baby clothes I had bought him didn't fit. He swam in them. The newborn disposable nappies were huge, the waist of them sitting just under his armpits. He was only just growing into these things now, at two months of age.

I had enjoyed turning our little cottage into a home. I started sewing and made some nice curtains and cushions for the living room. They were a navy and white check, which matched the new blue couch and white walls. I had left the old couch for Dean, I thought I should leave something for him to sleep on. Actually, I left the other one behind because it was falling apart. I didn't care whether Dean had anywhere to sleep at all. I bought the blue couch second-hand, it was almost new and was a steal at $100.

I was happy, comfortable and safe. The day we had moved I said my goodbyes to Fiona. We had become closer than I had realised. It was difficult saying goodbye to my only friend.

Three months to the day after Jack's birth, I received a summons to appear in the Family Law Court. Dean wanted visitation rights. I couldn't understand why. He had not seen his son once in three months, so why now? I knew it wouldn't have been merely out of concern. He hadn't been concerned before Jack was born. I couldn't see any reason why he should care now. He had shown Kate little affection in her first few years, other than in public; he didn't seem to care about her at all. I knew there must have been an ulterior motive for this latest move. I just didn't know what it was.

I saw a solicitor and applied for legal aid. I didn't have the money for representation any other way. I didn't know what to expect, but it certainly wasn't what I got.

The solicitor was an ageing, grey-haired, scrawny man. He reminded me of Mr Burns from 'The Simpsons'. The only difference was that Mr Henry Chapman was not a yellow cartoon character, and was not as feisty as the old cartoon man was.

Now I understood why legal aid was free. I was about to be screwed by the system again, one look at the shrinking man before me told me that. Shit. Shit. Shit.

My life had been so peaceful over the past three months. So happy and peaceful. I had been enjoying my children the way a mother should. Without being scared of what their father might do next. By the end of the hour-long appointment with Henry 'one foot in the grave' Chapman, I was more depressed than I had been since I received the summons.

We were due in court next week and this was my representation. Nothing, zilch, zip, zero.

There was nothing I could do to keep my babies away from Dean. Past criminal history was irrelevant. His vicious assaults on me were irrelevant. Past history could not be brought into it as it had no bearing on his ability to raise a child, according to the Family Court, and because it was a family law court its aim was to keep families together. In particular, parents and their children. I didn't disagree in principle. Children shouldn't be separated from loving parents.

My children had not suffered physically. Without physical scars I had no case. Dean would be granted visitation rights, the old man assured me of that. 'It is the law.' That was how he ended his tactless speech on fathers' rights.

'Too many women try to dispose of fathers easily. Only to replace them with a new one the next day.' He was glaring at me over the tops of his glasses.

I was heartbroken. How was I going to do it? How was I going to send my babies off with a madman? He may have contributed to their being, but he was no father.

A father is loving and kind, a father makes his children

feel special, more special and more loved than anyone in the world. A father makes his children's mother feel special. A father protects his children from evil, he doesn't introduce them to it.

The court case was a miserable affair. I spent the whole time wishing they would just speak English. I couldn't understand a word of their strange legal jargon. It made no sense at all. It was like they were speaking in secret code.

Dean was dressed in his court suit. It was the only time I ever saw him wear it. The same suit each and every court appearance, and he looked good in it. I wish I could lie, but he really did. No wonder he sucked people in so well. He knew exactly what he was doing. Unfortunately his good looks didn't travel to the inside, to the core. Dean had no heart.

The court had apparently ordered that 'the children spend each alternate weekend with their father'. Henry explained this to me. Dean was to pick Kate and Jack up from my home this coming Saturday. Dean now had my address and phone number, all granted within a matter of hours.

Today was Tuesday. At 10 o'clock on Saturday morning Dean would be at my house.

Dean pulled into my driveway at five minutes to ten on Saturday morning. I had dreaded this moment, hoping he wouldn't come, hoping that he really didn't want to see the kids. I had had no sleep the night before. Jack had never been away from me for more than a few hours, and he didn't know his father.

I didn't let Dean in, I made him stand at the screen door, only opening it when I was ready to hand over my small children. It was the hardest thing I had ever had to do. I had told myself not to cry. I didn't want Kate to see me upset. I tried to be happy for her. I tried speaking like I was happy. I tried smiling like I was happy. Kate hadn't wanted to go from the moment I had told her.

I felt as though I had let her down again. I had: I had let them both down. I'd promised to never leave them, that we would always be together – and I was sending them away. Sending Kate somewhere she didn't want to go. She had seen the destruction her father could cause. She knew she was being sent to hell and I could see the fear in her big blue eyes. There was nothing I could do. I had no choice.

I opened the door and kissed Jack's head, lingering, breathing his baby smell deeply, my eyes stinging. I handed him to Dean. I bent down and hugged Kate, kissing her on the forehead the same way I had done to her brother.

I wanted to tell her to be a good girl. I wanted to tell her that I loved her. I wanted to tell her that I would see her in her dreams, but I couldn't. The lump in my throat prevented me from speaking. If I had tried I would have broken down. So I said nothing, hating myself for not being able to, needing to hold on to my emotions. Needing to for Kate. I tried to smile and pat her on the arm affectionately. I watched from the open door as she walked off, with Dean holding Jack in his arms.

I wasn't sure how long I could manage to keep myself together. Kate half-turned and waved.

'I'll miss you, Mummy,' she called.

I waved back at her, still unable to speak. As she climbed into the back of the car Dean had acquired from somewhere, I could no longer take it. I began unravelling like a piece of cloth, strand by strand as I stood in my doorway watching the car reversing out of the driveway.

I let the door close itself and I turned and ran to my room, throwing myself onto the bed. I sobbed; I sobbed harder than I ever had before. I felt empty – empty and alone. How was I going to cope for the next 31 hours?

I cried for twelve of them before falling asleep and dreaming. Dreaming of children playing in streaks of golden light, calling me. Over and over again, calling me.

The following day I was still depressed and my eyes were puffy. The time dragged by. Mum had called; she and Dad were coming over for lunch. They were worried because they hadn't heard from me, so they would bring lunch and cheer me up. Good luck, I thought. I didn't think I could be cheered up. I didn't feel like company, but didn't have the strength to argue. They would have come anyway.

I was too preoccupied with the slow-moving hands on the clock to even carry out a decent conversation. It was only midday and there were still five hours to go until Dean brought Kate and Jack back.

I picked at the chicken and potato salad Mum had brought with her. I wasn't hungry and was too worried to try to eat.

'Have you finished?' Dad asked, taking my plate to finish off what I had left.

Mum started clearing the dishes from the little kitchen table I had brought from the other house. She took them to the kitchen, starting to stack them in the sink to be washed. She turned on the tap to fill the sink.

'Don't wash them, Mum, I'll do it.'

'It's okay,' she answered, sounding slightly offended, as if I'd implied she wasn't capable.

'No, Mum, really. It will give me something to do.' I needed to occupy myself somehow over the next few hours or I was going to go mad.

The closer the time drew to five o'clock the more anxious I became. My mountain cottage was so clean it sparkled by the time I heard a car pull into the driveway. I had cleaned the house from top to bottom, not because it was dirty, but because it passed the time. I scrubbed the tiled floors in the kitchen and bathroom. Vacuumed the carpet, finished the washing and polished anything that could be polished.

I couldn't wait for Katie's grubby little fingers to mark everything again. I hated it usually, following her around with a cloth. Now I missed it.

I ran to the front door. Kate was already there waiting for me. I opened the screen door and picked her up, twirling her around on the small verandah. I was so happy to see her. Dean brought Jack to me and I took my baby, holding him close, breathing in his baby smell as I'd done when I'd handed him over to Dean. I didn't speak to Dean – what was there to say?

I took my children inside and closed the door. Dean left their belongings on the step and I collected them after he had gone.

Kate and Jack slept in my bed that night. Kate insisted Jack be in the middle so she could cuddle him all night. I agreed with her as long as she let me cuddle them both. She giggled and so did I. Jack smiled up at us from his position in between mother and sister. We were together again, and I already dreaded our next separation. But there was no need. Dean didn't come to pick them up again.

Kate's third birthday came and went. Jack started to crawl and I got a part-time job at a local tourist destination. Kate and Jack were booked into day care three days a week while I worked in a kiosk serving busloads of noisy tourists.

During my lunch breaks I would sometimes find a bench to sit on outside and take in the majestic scenery. No matter where you are in these mountains you are always assured the most magnificent views – you don't have to look very far.

I loved working; I had enjoyed the part-time job I had as a teenager when I was at school. I liked meeting new people and making extra money.

Most of the money I earned now was spent on childcare. There wasn't much left over so I mainly worked for social interaction. It beat learning the alphabet over again and watching *Sesame Street* to the point where I could no longer stand the sight of Big Bird. It was so good to have other people to talk to, normal conversation, to be able to voice my own opinion, to be able to express my likes and dislikes without fear.

The kiosk was a busy place. We were constantly run off our feet. There were always people lined up outside waiting to get in and there were buses lined up in the massive circular driveway – it was a never-ending procession. There were tourists from every corner of the globe; I met so many different kinds of people.

I had re-joined the world and was having a ball. I worked with another girl who was only a few years older than me. We were the Monday, Wednesday and Friday girls. Kym and I had a system. Once I had the hang of what I was doing we were fast, serving buckets of hot chips, ready-made sandwiches, ice-creams, milkshakes and a variety of other snacks over the busy counter.

We laughed so much I thought my sides would split. Kym and I had fun working together but never spent time socialising after work. Kym was single and partied a lot. My current lifestyle was a little too sedate for her. Hell, it probably would have been for me if I hadn't been tied down with two kids.

Anyone who knew me at work also knew that I had kids but that was all they knew. I didn't talk about any other part of my life. Who wanted to hang around with a woman with two noisy kids when they were young? Not many people, I had found out. I had worked at the kiosk for five months and hadn't made any close friends. I had a good time with my co-workers, but only at work. Most of them hung out together after work, but not me. I went home to be with my children each night. Not alone, but lonely.

One evening the phone rang after I put Kate and Jack to bed. I expected it to be Mum or Dad as they were the only ones who ever called me.

'Hello, Amy.' It was Dean. I was so shocked I almost dropped the phone. I hadn't heard from him in months, not since his visit with the kids when Jack was only three months old. A lot of time had passed and I had heard nothing from him at all.

'What do you want, Dean?' I asked. I tried to keep my

voice strong and steady. My hands had begun to shake and I didn't want him to hear it in my voice.

'I want you.' He said this with a certain amount of confidence. It wasn't often that Dean didn't get what he wanted. It showed in his voice.

'Leave me alone.' I hung up before he had the chance to say anything else. My hands were now shaking uncontrollably. I went to the bathroom and splashed some cold water on my face. Its freshness, cooling me, stopped some of the hot panic that had begun to surface. I hadn't been this rattled for a long time. I dried my face and looked at myself in the mirror. The phone started ringing loudly again. I ran to the living room and picked it up, not wanting the children to wake up.

'Leave me alone,' I said without so much as a hello.

'Well, there is no need to be so rude, Amy.' Oh my God, it was Mum.

'Sorry, Mum, I – I didn't know it was you,' I stammered.

'Well, who did you think it was?'

I couldn't tell her Dean had just called as she would have been worried. I really had no idea what to say. I had no time to make up something. I couldn't think fast enough. I needed time to lie.

'Amy, what's going on?' I still had not answered her.

'Nothing, Mum. I'm just tired. I've had a really busy day. I just want to go to bed and collapse.' There, I hoped that would be enough to ease her concerns and give her the hint that I did not want to talk.

Luckily it worked. She told me to go straight to bed and get some rest and I promised that I would. Thoughts of Dean filled my head. The nice Dean, the disturbed Dean, the handsome Dean and the evil Dean were all tormenting me.

I got up and went into the dining room. I put on some music and listened to Freddie Mercury sing his greatest hits while I went through the kitchen cupboards, writing out my next shopping list. Anything to stop my mind whirling out of control. I finally managed to get to sleep at 3 a.m., restless.

Dean called again the next night and was much more persistent this time. Each time I hung up, he rang back. The last time I picked up the phone before disconnecting it from the wall he threatened to burn the house down while we slept. It wouldn't have been hard for him to make his way silently under the floor and light a fire. Kate, Jack and I would probably all be dead from smoke inhalation before the fire even took hold properly.

These thoughts freaked me out all night. I jumped at every sound, sitting in the dark. I had worked all day after a restless night's sleep. I was exhausted, yet I sat on the couch, eyes open, awake, alert.

I was so tired.

The next day I put kids' videos on and played them all day, while I slept on the floor, Jack jumping happily all over me. Both kids made me drag my tired limbs to the kitchen when they were thirsty or hungry. I felt half-dead.

That night the phone didn't ring and I fell asleep holding a knife under my pillow.

❧

The mornings I worked were always a mad rush. The alarm clock beeped me awake at 5.30 and I was in the shower, washing myself in record time, almost tripping over wrestling toddlers in the doorway. I would rip them apart and try to dress them. It was a major feat, dressing a child who is desperate to escape your grasp and run away from you laughing. It is extremely frustrating when there is a time limit involved. I would finish making the lunches and organise breakfast.

I was finally sitting at the table with my morning cup of tea. Jack was in his highchair feeding himself mashed cereal and Kate was sitting up at the table eating toast and jam. I was thinking of the things I still needed to put in the day care bag, like extra nappies, when we heard a loud bang come from somewhere. We heard another sound seconds later, louder, that sounded like a bomb blast. I got up and went to the hallway while the kids looked at me, shock plain to see on their little round faces.

As soon as I entered the narrow hall, Dean appeared. I started walking slowly backwards in the direction I had come. It was stupid, I should have let him follow me into another room, not where the kids were, but my brain wasn't thinking. I did what was instinctive.

'Mummy?' I heard a puzzled Kate say as she saw me entering the room backwards.

'It's okay, darling.' I tried to keep my voice calm. 'Kate, get Jack for me and sit with him on the floor.' I spoke slowly, my eyes keeping contact with Dean's cold, soulless eyes. Once his eyes had been a vibrant blue, like the sky on a brilliant summer's day. Now they were dark and dull, like the gloomy depths of the ocean, empty and cold.

I heard Kate move. She was talking to Jack. I couldn't make out what she was saying. I could only hear her faint voice as she helped Jack out of the highchair. As Dean's large foreboding figure came through the door Kate screamed. His eyes shot in her direction, fixing on her.

'Leave her alone, Dean.' My voice was strong. 'It's me you want.'

His eyes flew back my way, flashing an evil glare.

'That's right. It is you I want,' he paused. His voice was deep, low, and barely audible. 'That's why I'm staying. We're going to be a happy family.'

'No, you're not.' He really had gone mad! I couldn't believe what he was saying. 'I can have you arrested for being here now, Dean.'

'No, you won't.' He hadn't moved any further towards me. His voice hadn't changed. 'You won't be telling anyone. No-one will know I'm here. Will they, Amy.' He wasn't asking me, he was telling me.

'Try and stop me, Dean.' I was challenging him. I knew

from past experience that this was a mistake, but it was also a mistake giving in to him without a fight. The treatment didn't change much anyway, no matter which path you chose to take.

He made his move. Charging toward me like a raging bull. It would only take him a few large strides to reach me; I stepped back once, then twice. Something went wrong. I stepped on a toy that had been left on the floor and my ankle buckled, causing me to lose my balance. I tumbled to the floor, landing on the small plastic Fisher-Price car. I tried to get up, wincing at the pain in my right ankle. Dean's large foot clad in steel-capped leather work boots connected with my shoulder, kicking me back to the floor.

Jack was crying hysterically and I saw Katie drag him, still in a sitting position, nappy sliding across the floor. She dragged him into the corner of the room and crouched down with him, hugging him tightly.

'Will you shut up!' Dean yelled so loud, head turned to the corner where Kate had taken Jack for refuge. His yelling only resulted in Jack's crying increasing in volume. Dean turned on his heel and stormed into the kitchen, finding the cutlery drawer. While he rummaged through it I tried once more to lift myself from the cold floor.

Within a minute Dean was flying across the floor in front of me with a carving knife held firmly in his hand. He was heading toward the kids. I got up, no longer feeling my ankle and launched myself at him. It was a tackle any footballer would be proud of; I knocked him right off his feet, both of us crashing to the floor. He hadn't seen me coming. I had taken him by surprise. I looked for the knife, which had been in his hand. I had heard it slide across the floor, I needed to get it before he did.

I couldn't see it. My eyes scanned the floor, my body straining to recover before Dean did but I was too slow; he was up before me, grabbing me and dragging me up with him.

'You leave my kids alone, Dean. If you touch them I will kill you, I swear I will.' I wasn't scared, I spoke firmly again as he held tightly onto my arm. I felt no fear.

'Well, they're not only your kids, are they?' he said into my ear. 'And I can touch them if I want to, just like I touch you. Because I want to.'

'Just kill me if you want to, Dean, but don't touch them. That's all I ask.'

'Kill you?' he laughed, as though I had said something funny. 'Oh, I don't want to kill you. Well, not yet anyway. I want to torture you first. I want to hear you scream for mercy.'

He picked me up and lifted me over his head as you would a bar of weights. It all happened so fast, before I knew it I had hit the wall and was lying at the bottom on the cold floor once more. That was all I could feel, the cold tiles against flesh. There was no pain, just cold hardness. Kate and Jack were now both sobbing, squashed back as far as they could go into the corner.

I was looking at them not realising that Dean was standing above me. He plucked me from the floor and slammed my back against the wall, the back of my head hitting it hard. Still I felt no pain – just sensations, but no pain. Dean bent his head close to mine.

'See what I can do to you, Amy?' He sounded smug.

'Nothing you can do can hurt me.' I looked at him with eyes blackened by as much red hatred as his own.

'Don't you think so?' One of his hands quickly wrapped around my throat, squeezing, relaxing, squeezing, and relaxing. 'Let's see,' he added.

I was standing with my back against the wall; I started to feel my body slide upwards, my feet leaving the ground. He was pushing me up the wall holding me by the throat. It was getting harder to breathe. I looked at my babies huddled in the corner. Dean noticed my eyes change direction and followed my gaze.

'I know.' Dean spoke suddenly. 'I know how to hurt you. I'll kill them in front of you. I'll make you watch, maybe I'll even make you join in.' He spoke as though he was thinking out loud, giving voice to a new, sick fantasy.

He looked at me long and hard. My breathing was growing shallow, my head light, vision beginning to blur. My eyes were fixed firmly on my tiny children, terrified in the corner.

At that moment I really thought I was going to die. My babies' faces began to fade and I blacked out.

I woke up in my bed, my throat sore, flesh tender. It was light outside. I couldn't remember anything. I turned my head and looked at the door – it was closed. My body ached but I could hear Kate's faint laugh travelling to me from beyond the door.

I sat up slowly, painfully grabbing my head, which was throbbing. I felt a lump on the back of my skull the size of a golf ball. I was confused.

'Dean,' I whispered.

Reality came back to me with the force of a rushing waterfall, showering me in memory. The door opened and my eyes flew sharply in that direction, head pounding at the swift movement. Dean stood in the doorway, smiling. He closed the door gently behind him and came to sit on the bed next to me. My mind was numb.

'Your boss has been told you won't be going back to work, so you don't have to worry about that,' he began as if he had done me a favour by giving me one less thing to worry about. 'We are both going to sort everything out, okay?' he continued. 'I love you, Amy. I wish you would understand that.'

He was looking at me, smiling. It was a strange smile. He had gone crazy, had always been crazy. I wanted to ask him about Kate and Jack but I couldn't speak. I couldn't make my brain respond. They must have been fine because I could hear them playing, their voices growing louder.

'You go back to sleep, I'll look after the kids.' He kissed my forehead. I could practically feel my skin begin to bubble and burn beneath his vile touch.

I had woken up stuck in some weird nightmare. As I lay myself back down again the protests made by my body with every move told me this was no dream.

I had to think. I had to get out of this. The police hadn't helped at all in the end. What good was a stupid piece of paper with the words 'restraining order' written on it now? What good was it doing for me?

I had to think. I had to win this game. Phase three of the plan from long ago was about to be put in place. I would bide my time and find the help I needed. It was my turn to smile. I lay in bed and smiled at the stark white ceiling. I may have looked broken, but was far from it.

He could break my body, but not my spirit and not my soul. These were things I would never let him take from me. Never again would I let him take the two things I could refuse him control of.

So the game had begun once more, and I was determined to win this round. Dead or alive, I would win.

My plan was working a treat. I played the depressed, pathetic woman who needed antidepressants, and needed

Dean. He seemed to enjoy it. He seemed to enjoy the fact that I was, so he thought, more pathetic and crazy than he was.

He enjoyed taking me to the doctor and explaining what he thought was wrong with me because I had refused to speak since I had woken up.

I think Dean was most impressed that all his hard work had finally paid off. I had finally cracked; he had finally sent me insane. I would pick my moments to do strange things – never when the kids were around. Dean didn't ever seem to notice this.

I would sit on the floor, knees up to my chin, my arms locked together around my legs, and rock back and forth. I mostly did this at night when the kids were asleep. I would rock and moan, moan and rock. My performances were fantastic, very convincing, worthy of an Oscar.

I was worried that if I carried these episodes on too long I would go crazy. It was maddening, not speaking and staring into space for hours. But I needed to be patient, I had to take my time if I was going to make this work, and it would work; I was going to make sure of it. It didn't matter what I had to do – it would all be worth it in the end.

Dean would bring the antidepressants to me and I would pretend to take them like a good girl. I would stash them underneath the mattress when he had left the room. As soon as my body had healed properly and I had enough pills hidden away I could make my move.

Things carried on this way for the next three weeks. I could walk on my ankle with little pain and my pill pile was growing. It had been a real feat trying to keep Mum and Dad away. Whenever Dean left the house I gave them a call. I made up excuses for not seeing them. My plan was that if I called them as often as I could, then they wouldn't feel the need to call here. So far so good. Everything was going well.

I started to recover from my pretend illness. Doing small things like washing and cooking dinner and making beds. I started making a habit of preparing Dean a marshmallow-topped hot chocolate while he watched television every night. Before I went to bed I would take the steaming mug to him.

I still didn't speak. I was too worried about saying the wrong thing and ruining my plans. I didn't want to stuff up after I had come this far.

Dean did most things for the children while I suffered my temporary insanity. He did a lot of things I didn't like. If Kate wanted lollies for breakfast, Dean gave her lollies. I said nothing. I had to keep my mouth shut to be able to get through this. I spent a lot of time biting my tongue.

Over the preceeding days when Dean left the house to pick something up from the shop, I had run around packing pieces of clothing into plastic bags, hiding them under the house. Over four days I had packed as many things as I could without Dean noticing.

On the fourth night I made Dean the usual frothy, marshmallow-topped chocolate drink. Only this time I added the magic ingredient, the pile of little white pills I had collected. I tasted it to make sure it hadn't altered. Then I added another teaspoon of chocolate and one of sugar, just to be sure, and I put an extra marshmallow on top.

With the hot mug in my hands I took a deep breath, and closing my eyes I said a silent prayer before going into the living room with the drink. I handed it to Dean, smiling my sweetest smile.

I sat, and I waited.

It didn't take as long as I thought it would for the drugs to take effect. I hadn't bothered to count the number of tablets I had put into the drink. I watched him closely as he drained the last of the chocolate liquid. Dean started to get up.

'Man, I feel like shit.' He stood up, trying to keep his balance. He looked drunk. He took wobbly steps to the doorway and turned the corner, heading into the dining room, no longer in view.

I heard a giant thud. I stayed still, waiting a moment, listening for more sounds. There was nothing, only silence. I walked cautiously to the doorway and looked around the corner.

Dean was lying on his stomach on the dining room tiles, his huge body sprawled out on the floor. I stood there waiting for him to move. I took a hesitant step forward.

'Jesus, Amy, this is what you've waited for. It worked. So move!' I screamed to myself. I couldn't believe it had happened. I took another step closer, then another. I looked closely at his face with thoughts of everything he had done to me, every torturous touch, every evil word.

The hatred I felt for him grew. I kicked him gently with my foot. No movement. I kicked him again, harder. Still no sign of consciousness, only the slow rise of his chest as he breathed.

'I beat you, Dean,' I said, looking down on him. 'This time I beat you.' I kicked him again, as hard as I could, right in his ribs.

I spent the next 45 minutes running around the house, grabbing things I hadn't been able to pack already. More clothes, nappies, baby bottles, photos, food and favourite toys. I ran in and out of the house, piling things into the car. Ironically, Dean had trained me for this; I laughed at the memory of running from the house in Clairvale trying to see how many stolen goods we could fit in the car.

Finally I lifted my sleeping children from their beds and fled into the night. I didn't look back once.

PART 2

Choices

Chapter 8

I drove all night, stopping only for coffee, Coke and toilets. Kate and Jack slept in their seats in the back of the car. The boot was filled with clothing and toiletries, photo albums and toys. In the front seat sat an Esky with milk and juice for the kids should they wake up in between towns. There was also the shoebox containing my old ballet shoes, all that was left of the old Amy. This would be the one thing that would remain with me forever. My only link to past happiness.

Most of the vehicles on the road were trucks, huge semitrailers, all heading north. I was following them to Queensland. My parents had no idea what had happened over the past month and they had no idea what I was doing or where I was going now. They had thought that if I lived closer to them they could protect me. The police thought they could protect me. The reality was that nobody could. I had to rely on myself and I would do whatever I had to do to stay alive.

I knew this wasn't going to be completely over just because I had left. Dean would come looking for me – I knew that. He was going to be rather pissed off about what I had done to him. I smiled at the memory while I drove down the highway. I opened the window as far as it would go and the cold air whipped my face, making me feel alive. I looked down at the glowing numbers on the dash. It was 3 a.m. I had been driving for five hours. I wondered how many hours it would take to get to the border. I had no idea how far it was. I wasn't tired; adrenalin was still keeping me alert.

I had been acting like I had brain damage for weeks, planning this little adventure. I would have to stop somewhere in the morning and call my parents. I felt guilty for not letting them know what had happened.

I travelled with the trucks all night. By the time the sun started to come up I was getting tired. It was going to be hard; I didn't know where I was going to stop. Jack was becoming restless in the back seat. I looked for signs to the next town. I had no idea where I was; I had never heard of most of the towns I had driven through. I was excited and scared. I hadn't really put much thought into what I was going to do after drugging Dean, other than leaving and driving away as fast as I could.

I decided that once I had reached the next town I would find a motel room – at least there would then be a television to keep the kids amused. My plan had originally been to stop at a caravan park, which was the cheaper option, but there would be no television. Kids' television finished at midday, so that would give me a few hours' rest.

It was 9.30 when we let ourselves into the cheap motel room. I could see why it was so inexpensive. It smelled musty. The carpet was old and worn, brown and patchy, dark stains showing. The double bed was covered with an ugly green floral bedspread. There were matching floral curtains hanging over the small windows and even if they had been open I doubt that any light would have shone through the small squares. The walls hadn't been painted in a long time. The once cream paint was now grubby and flaky.

I walked to the door on the opposite side of the room. Inside was a tiny bathroom with a shower in one corner and toilet and small basin squashed in the other. There was barely enough room to open the door all the way. The tiles were small, a similar colour brown to the carpet. Many were missing.

'Oh well.' I shrugged, walking back into the other room and turning the television on for Kate and Jack, who were playing on the floor with the toys they had brought in from the car. I found a channel that would keep them amused – B1 and B2 were getting up to their crazy tricks on 'Bananas in Pyjamas'. As the kids played I fell asleep, exhausted from the long drive. It had certainly been an eventful 24 hours.

I was woken a couple of hours later by Jack trying to lift my eyelids open by the lashes. He had climbed on the bed and was sitting next to my head trying to force my eyes open.

'What do you want, Jack?' I croaked, not ready to wake up. I felt like I had been drinking and was hungover. My head was heavy from the exhausting night. It is amazing how tired driving that distance can make you. I was wrecked.

'He wants a drink, Mummy.' Kate answered from her position on the end of the bed watching telly. She always answered for him, Jack only had to grunt and Kate seemed to know exactly what he needed or wanted.

I usually told her not to speak for him, as he needed to learn how to communicate for himself. Kate persisted, though, and I was too tired to say anything about it this time.

I opened my eyes with difficulty so Jack would leave them alone and I pulled his head down, biting his neck softly, causing a mass of riotous laughter.

'Me too, Mummy, me too.' Kate was now on the other side of me, bouncing on her knees on the lumpy mattress. I grabbed her also and smothered them with a thousand kisses, tickling them as I went. Their laughter filled the room and I joined them. The three of us laughing and laughing until I couldn't take it any more. I was out of breath and I thought my sides were going to split. Jack forgot about the drink he had wanted and we lay on the bed, each half of my heart wrapped securely in my arms.

Kate asked when we were going home and I didn't know what to say. I kissed the top of her head and just lay there staring at the rotting motel ceiling.

That afternoon I called my parents. I was spending that night in the same motel room; I would drive again in the morning. I needed a full night's sleep.

'Amy, thank God,' Mum sounded panicked. 'Where are you? We've been worried sick.' She was speaking so fast I could hardly keep up with her. 'What was Dean doing in your house?' She threw another question at me.

I explained everything to her. Well, not everything, but everything she needed to know.

She despised Dean almost as much as I did.

I told her that I wouldn't be speaking to her again for a while, that it would be safer for them if I didn't. I had met a lot of the men Dean had spent time with in prison. None seemed afraid of going back inside and were quite often thinking up new ways of making their dreams come true. They were proud of doing time and bragged about it constantly. They liked to talk about their crimes. I knew it might not be just Dean I would be hiding from. Some of these people could fix you up so that you would never speak again.

The conversation ended with us both crying. Mum was

finding this harder than I was. I had had years to prepare for this inevitable moment. She had minutes.

The takeaway shop was only a few doors away from the motel. I hadn't had any room left in the car for the stroller, but because it was so close we walked, Jack waddling some of the way, me carrying him the rest. I bought some fish and chips and a bottle of apple juice.

We started our short walk back, Jack in my arms carrying the juice. Kate was walking beside me holding the bag with the fish and chips. She asked again when we were going home. I didn't know how I was supposed to approach her question. What could I say that a three-and-a-half-year-old would understand?

'Do you want to go home to Daddy?' I asked her gently.

'Daddy's a bad man,' she said, looking straight ahead, a strong furrow formed in her brow.

Luckily Kate was sidetracked by a lady beetle crawling along the footpath in front of her. She picked up the tiny, brightly-coloured beetle between her fingers and moved it to the grassy area at the side of the path, pleased with herself because now the little bug would not get stepped on.

We ate our dinner back in the musty, drab motel room. Once both children were cleaned up they lay in the big bed watching television. It wasn't long before they drifted off into peaceful sleep.

I sat at the small writing desk and rolled a joint. I had taken Dean's marijuana bag before leaving the house. That would really annoy him. It had only been an afterthought as I ran out the door, but I was glad I'd done it. I could do with the relief and relaxation it would bring.

I sat in the small bathroom and lit the joint, breathing its heavy smoke into my lungs. My head and limbs were beginning to feel the effects, growing heavier with each toke. Once it was finished I went back into the main room where the kids slept and sat back down at the desk.

I picked up the pen and wrote to my parents. The phone call hadn't been easy, and was not enough. I couldn't say the things I had wanted to say. It was far too emotional. So I wrote to them, to describe my feelings the best way I could.

Dear Mum and Dad,

There is nothing I can do. And nothing I can say, to make all your troubles go away.

I am helping myself, the best way I can. Alone and scared is all that I am.

The devil wants to play; I must keep him at bay. I only wish I knew the way.

There are two little treasures that I must keep near. It is them that help me stay focused and clear.

All I ask is a life full of laughter and cheer. Where pain and sorrow no longer come near.

The life that leads me is killing me slow. The help that I seek is nowhere, you know.

I know you will miss me. I will miss you too. But it won't be forever, that I assure you.

I don't give up easily. You know I never have. I must continue to live. And learn to be brave.

Look in the night sky and pick us a star. Then you will remember we are not so very far.

Love forever. Amy

Kate and Jack too.

It was hard to write. I began to feel myself start to fall apart. I sat up straight and took a deep breath; I needed to keep myself together. No more tears. No more fear. Survival would rule. Raw instinct. Feelings, thoughts and memories would need to be discarded. I needed to find strength, become hardened and tough. Or I would never survive.

While my heart walked on the outside, what began to form in its place was a solid callus, which could not be penetrated. It would now be impossible for anyone to enter the locked room that contained my feelings. Only my children held the key.

I folded the letter and placed it in the envelope. I would post it in the morning. With heavy eyes, I climbed into the big lumpy bed and slept.

We were up early in the morning, driving once again, heading north, making our way to the Sunshine State. We had only been driving for a couple of hours when we crossed the border at Tweed Heads. I wasn't going to stop.

I was going to keep driving and see where the road would take me.

Whenever Kate and Jack started to get restless I looked out for rest areas and parks along the roadside. I passed lots of stalls selling all the tropical fruits I loved but could usually never afford to buy. There were mangoes and avocadoes, very cheap. I decided to stop at the next one and introduce Kate and Jack to these exotic fruits. They loved the mangoes, the juice dripping from their chins. The avocadoes they weren't too fussed on, though.

I wasn't sure what we were going to do that night, but I wouldn't worry about that yet. The temperature changed dramatically the further on we went. Kate and Jack now sat in their seats only wearing underwear and I wished I could do the same. All the windows had been wound down, though it made little difference as the wind was hot. I didn't know which was better, the hot car or the hot wind.

I had stopped for more ice to fill the Esky with, not only to keep our drinks cool, but also to prevent the kids from overheating. I threw handfuls of ice into the back seat for them. They thought it was hilarious. Kate couldn't believe it! Mum was making a mess! Mum didn't care. Mum was having fun, a rare sight indeed.

I was bopping along to the music on the radio, singing away to the songs. After a while they both joined in, although they weren't singing any words you could understand. I didn't even think they were words, just noises. I felt free, like a huge weight had been lifted from my shoulders.

We stopped often to stretch our legs. There were lots of places to pull over. Some of the roadside rest areas were very nice, like little park areas with amenities and wooden bench seats and tables. There were also water tanks filled with rainwater so you could replenish your own supply from the tap.

Some rest areas weren't so nice, however, and were obviously a lot older. The tables and benches were rotting away, barely standing. There was no grass, only gravel like a parking area. We didn't stop at these for long, and only if we really had to, for instance if Jack had dirtied his nappy and was stinking us out of the car. Then we had no choice.

We started staying in caravan parks. Camping would have been much cheaper. But there would have been so many other things to get – a tent didn't have anywhere to cook food and I didn't have the room to cart extra things around, anyway. So I would have to stick to caravans and hope that I could find parks with vacancies every night.

I was still getting welfare payments so I could afford cheap accommodation, petrol and food. I wasn't doing too badly, really, and I was seeing and doing things I normally would not have done. Going places I normally would not have gone.

The kids became very excited when we drove past cows and sheep grazing in their paddocks – they had never seen these things in the open before, only in pictures in books or on television.

When we got to Brisbane, I drove right through the busy city. I wanted to stay away from the cities, the crowds, the people and the cars. We made our way upthe north coast to Cairns then across to the Red Centre, the outback.

It was the most rugged, yet one of the most beautiful places I had ever seen. The terrain is flat, spread across the horizon. You can see forever. Here is where you realise how vulnerable you are, how insignificant, a speck on this vast dusty expanse.

The star-filled nights were an amazing sight. I had never seen so many stars; the sky had never looked so big. I had seen lots of photos and documentaries on television about the Australian centre, but nothing compared to being here. Nothing prepares you for its harshness, and its beauty.

Kate and Jack began to look like feral children, covered in thick red dust that was impossible to remove from their clothes. It seemed to embed itself in every fibre. It ended up in everything. It even managed to stain skin. I lived in a bikini and sarong; it was too hot for anything more. I had never felt heat like this. For the first time in my life I was tanning. I didn't think it was possible. Usually I turned into a lobster, but I was going brown. The kids were almost black – since they had their father's skin it didn't take long.

It was hard to cool down. There was really nowhere to swim, you couldn't just jump into any inviting pool of water. And you couldn't forget that, or a crocodile might just eat you. I had heard a story about a couple of campers who had pitched their tent by the riverbank and one had gone into the water. Surprisingly, the guy in the water was the one who watched his mate being gobbled up on the riverbank before his eyes. And I always thought you would have been safer out of the water. That goes to show how much I know.

We passed many squashed snakes along the way; some were almost as long as the car. It was a frightening sight. Who knew where these snakes were lurking when they weren't dead? One caravan park that I stayed at gave me a brochure upon arrival with a leaflet warning of the dangers of these snakes if you have toddlers. They are a good size for a snake's meal.

Needless to say, I kept a very close eye on Kate and little Jack. I did not want to see them become snake bait.

Chapter 9

Six months went by. We had made our way up to Darwin and then back down, cutting through the centre of our enormous island home, straight down through the Northern Territory to the bottom of South Australia, taking in the different sceneries along the way. The South Australian desert quickly turned into lush green fields.

We moved on, across to Victoria, and ended up in the picturesque town of Greens Park. It was a lovely little country town. We had been there a couple of days, staying in the local tourist park, when I noticed in the paper there were a number of farmhouses for rent for only $35 a week.

There's no harm in looking, I thought, circling a couple of the phone numbers. I was going to have to find somewhere to stop soon or I was going to end up back in New South Wales, which is not where I wanted to be. It would be nice to live in a house again.

The next day Kate, Jack and I went to look at one of the properties just outside the tiny town of Chifley. Chifley was a very small town: there were plenty of shopfronts but most had closed down over the years as people began to move to the cities in search of work. The only establishments that remained open were a service station, a milk bar selling general grocery items, and the pub. Apparently Chifley had been a bustling sheep town once, not too long ago; the locals often reminisced about the old times, the busy times.

The first house we saw was massive: three huge bedrooms, two living areas and an old kitchen with an adjoining sunroom. All this for only $35 a week – in Sydney you would pay at least $300 a week for a house this size. The view from every full-length window was amazing: gorgeous rolling green hills. You could see for miles, trees were scarce and there was nothing else around apart from the sheep and cows that grazed in the surrounding paddocks. I didn't mind sharing space with them.

The house was off the main road, down a long dirt driveway. There were two big water tanks and a freshwater creek running down the rear of the property, parallel to the house.

'I want this room, Mummy,' Kate called, running through the house, Jack close behind.

'Eh, she's keen,' the farmer chuckled. He had introduced himself as Dennis Smith; he was a stocky man, my height, wearing dirty jeans, leather boots, a flannelette shirt and an Akubra hat. He had a kind face and came across as a real country bumpkin. This house had belonged to his parents before they passed away. If Dennis couldn't find someone to rent and maintain it the house would only fall down, as so many others in the area had done. Dennis and his wife, Robyn, lived a couple of kilometres away on the extensive property that had been in the Smith family for generations. 'Farmin's in the blood,' as Dennis put it.

Kate, Jack and I moved into the old house only three days later. I purchased a few second-hand items from a furniture shop in Greens Park. Each week I got something different. It was a very mismatched but comfortable farmhouse. It was in the middle of nowhere and I loved it.

I loved the peace, the quietness. The only sounds came from the cattle. You wouldn't think cattle could be noisy, but they can, and they drove me crazy at first. Then, as with everything, I grew used to it. I grew to love the cows. If you look closely, they have very cute faces.

The kids and I went for daily walks. Lambing season was exciting for the kids; they loved to see all the baby sheep. We would go on missions to see how many we could count and if there were any new ones.

We would often go to the shearing sheds to watch the sheep being shorn. This was another highlight of farm life for Kate and Jack. They would both get a piece of the smelly wool to take home with them.

I liked country people. They kept to themselves and

seemed to have hearts of gold. Dennis would sometimes bring me meat he had left over from a slaughter. Sometimes he would bring me an entire side of beef. I have to say I found it difficult to eat, but did not wish to refuse such kindness. It was hard to eat animals that surrounded you, lived so close to you. I had become a friend to the cows. I couldn't eat them.

I kept mostly to myself; I hadn't spoken to many people, other than those I had to, for almost a year. I had been living in the farmhouse for five months when I figured I could take loneliness no longer. To begin with I had needed it. It had been therapeutic, just my kids and my thoughts. I didn't want to have to dodge people's questions and I knew I could not answer them truthfully.

Now I was getting lonely, no longer content with child conversations and deep and meaningfuls with friendly cows. I wanted company. I wanted to socialise. I wanted a job!

I scoured the Greens Park paper weekly for job vacancies that might suit me. Greens Park was a 45-minute drive away from the farmhouse and was the closest place I could work. I thought that once I had found employment I could move closer to town.

Kate and Jack were watching a Wiggles video while I sat with the paper and a coffee one Wednesday morning. There was a loud knock on the door; I was startled, spilling a mouthful of hot coffee down the front of my shirt.

'Shit.' No-one ever came here other than farmer Dennis

and he was here yesterday. He never came twice in one week. I wondered with a little apprehension about who it could be. The knock came again, stronger this time.

'Mummy. Who is it?' Kate turned to look at me, a frown covering her face, the knocking obviously interrupting her viewing.

I got up from the cheap brown-fabric-covered armchair and went to the door. A man stood on the other side, a stranger.

'Amy Marshall?' he asked as I opened the door fully.

'Um. Y-yes,' I answered hesitantly. Who the hell was he? He was middle-aged, dressed in beige slacks and a black jumper.

'Here you go.' He handed me a large white envelope.

'What's this?' I asked, confused.

'It's a summons to appear in court.' He turned and walked along the rocky path to his late-model four-wheel drive.

I went back to my spot in the living room. Kate and Jack were now dancing to their favourite Wiggles song. I opened the envelope and read its contents carefully.

Chapter 10

I moved out of the farmhouse, sold the furniture back to the shop I had purchased it from and made my way back to New South Wales.

Dennis and Robyn Smith sent us off warmly with a hug each and a homemade apple pie. I had every intention of coming back to Victoria after this was over. I liked it; it was a much cheaper place to live compared to my home state.

I arrived at my parents' house sixteen hours later. Kate and Jack were grumpy and I was exhausted. I was due in the Family Court in five days. Dean was taking me to court for breaching the previous order that had been made; he wanted his visitation rights reinstated.

Kate still had nightmares about 'the bad man cutting her head off'. Sometimes she watched my and Jack's heads being lopped off before losing her own. She was terrified.

I quite often sat with her all night while she cried, jumping at every sound. Kate was terrified of her father. I didn't ever say anything to her. I said nothing about Dean; I just listened to her. Little girls' dreams should consist of fairies and princesses, not knives and blood. I didn't talk to her but I usually cried with her.

Mum had arranged an appointment for me with a solicitor, who I saw the day after my arrival. It was the same old story. Dean had rights. This solicitor, although younger than the last one, still seemed hopeless. I guessed the dark-haired Mr John Maloney sitting before me would have been a handsome man in his younger days. He was probably in his mid to late fifties and had that look about him, distinguished.

'You have no proof of violence against yourself or the children. All you have is a black mark against you before you've even begun. You breached a previous visitation order and left the state.'

'Yes, but I explained why.' This Dean Martin look-alike was going to do nothing to help. I don't know why I was surprised, but I always was. Instead of tears, I wanted to burst into hysterical laughter at how much of a crock the legal system is. It's just a bunch of big words that normal people are flat out understanding, and these nobs go to school for years to learn how to mess you around, lie and play with your mind. They feed on your hopes and shatter them like brittle bones.

'And your other problem is your ex-partner's damning

statement. He claims,' he began, shuffling through a pile of papers. 'Ah. Here we are. He claims that you are a drug addict, partaking in the use of amphetamines. He claims you are an alcoholic and that you used to go on drinking binges for days at a time, leaving the children in his care.' He looked up at me, his eyebrows slightly raised.

I was completely astonished. 'For a start,' I began, 'the only time I wasn't in the house with my children was when he locked me out. I smoke a bit of pot every now and then. I do not take hard drugs. Dean is the one who sticks needles in his arms, not me. And I am not an alcoholic and the children have never been left with him.' My anger had begun to build steadily as I defended his accusations.

'Let me just say this. If this case consists of a slanging match, with him saying one thing and you saying another, it is highly likely the court will find you both unfit and remove the children from you. They may well find you unfit anyway because you have not been able to provide a very stable environment for the children, have you? Travelling around the country with them.' He was shaking his head.

The look on my face must have told him what I was thinking.

'Look,' he sighed, 'all you can do is go in there and agree to visitation. If you want to move interstate you will have to ask permission. He has to agree.'

'He won't ever agree with anything I want,' I said glumly, then continued, 'How can I trust him with the kids? You haven't seen it. Why don't you ask Kate what she wants?'

'Because she is too young, and who is to say you haven't put certain information into her head? That is how the courts will look at it.'

So once again I had to leave my children's fate to other people.

Kate and Jack were happy to see my parents again. It was like they had never been apart; they just picked up where they left off. They hadn't seen each other for eighteen months but had spoken on the phone regularly. The four of them had an amazing bond; it was special, closer than my relationship with my own grandparents.

Both of my sisters had now moved out of home. They weren't doing anything much with their lives, they were just happy to be out. I had been the same and now I wished I could turn back time and stay at home with Mum and Dad where it is safe and warm.

Mum came with me to court while Dad looked after Kate and Jack. The entrance to the Family Court building was like an airport: there were big metal detectors to walk through and X-ray machines for bags and other belongings, designed to keep weapons from the building.

John Maloney was waiting for us inside. Dean was at

the far end of the room wearing his usual court suit, chatting to his smartly dressed female solicitor.

Mum wasn't able to come into the courtroom as only Dean, the solicitors and myself were permitted. I was disappointed. I wanted her with me. I needed her with me.

I followed John Maloney into the large room and sat where he indicated. Dean and his solicitor sat to the right of us, Dean looking smug as always. I didn't look at him again throughout the proceedings. I was treated pretty much as I thought I would be. I nearly fell off the chair when the judge turned to address me after all the introductory jargon was out of the way.

'You, miss, are not in a favourable position. You will be lucky to leave here with anything less than 40 years' gaol. One year for every week you denied your children their father. It is behaviour I do not condone.'

His words were harsh and I couldn't believe he was telling me I was looking at spending half of my life in prison. For what? For protecting myself, and protecting my kids.

The beady-eyed judge dressed in his dark robes continued to read the statement provided by me and the one that listed Dean's twisted version of events.

'Right,' the judge looked up, resting his gaze heavily on me, then moving to Dean. 'I will never get to the bottom of this. I am writing out a proposal for each side and both of you must agree or suffer the consequences.

And, Miss Marshall,' he looked back in my direction. 'You have already been informed of what those consequences are likely to be. I am adjourning this case for two hours. I expect to see two signed pieces of paper when we reconvene. Do I make myself clear?'

I nodded. I didn't dare argue. At this point anything would be preferable to wasting away in gaol. Minutes later I was ushered out of the room to where Mum waited. John Maloney took us both to a small room with a table and chairs. We all sat down around the table as the solicitor explained everything that had happened and handed me the proposal in the judge's messy handwriting, after briefly going through it.

From what I understood, access was to begin immediately. The kids were to spend the next two weeks with Dean. He would then have them every second weekend and for half of every school holiday. If I moved back to Victoria then he would have to reimburse my travel costs to get them to New South Wales. As if he would ever do that, I thought. I was obligated to let him know our address and phone number, which in itself made me feel uneasy.

Mum took in more than I did. I was shocked. I had to agree to this and I didn't want to. Kate and Jack would have to be taken to Dean's mother's house the next day. That was where he was living at the moment, apparently. I didn't know why he had moved out of the Clairvale house and I didn't care. I should have been thankful the kids were going to Sharon's, but for two weeks! It was going to be hard. Jack didn't know them and I kept wondering how I was going to tell Kate.

I don't remember signing the order, nor do I remember going to lunch with Mum. I remember nothing more about that day apart from wanting to get back to my children and hug them so tight it wouldn't be possible to extract them from my arms.

That night after dinner I lay in bed with Kate and Jack reading *Jack and the Beanstalk*. Kate loved this story; it was her current favourite. They giggled every time Jack's name was mentioned.

'Who's that, Jack?' Kate would ask her brother while she pointed to the drawing of the fairytale Jack on the page. After the story I told them what was going to happen in the morning. Jack didn't really understand. Kate did, though.

'No. I'm not going.' Her arms were crossed. Kate was very strong-willed, always had been, and it was getting worse the older she became.

'I know you don't want to go, Katie, but you have to. The judge said so.'

'You can't make me.' Her arms were still folded across her chest, though her face had changed. Her expression softened, the frown fading. Lakes were forming under the big blue circles in her eyes, overflowing in tiny droplets onto her soft cheeks.

'No, Mummy,' she said. The waterfall began. I held out my arms, she climbed over to me and I encircled her in my embrace. A lump had formed in my throat and I was afraid to speak. I knew if I tried I would fall apart. I didn't want her to see my fear, though I am sure she sensed it.

The three of us slept in the single bed in my youngest sister's old room, knowing the morning would come.

I went alone to drop Kate and Jack at Sharon's house. I didn't want anyone to come with me. I wanted to be alone on the drive back. I had become used to my own company after living on the farm and I needed to be by myself.

Sharon greeted us at the door as if it were old times. The last time I had seen her I was pregnant with Jack, but you wouldn't have thought any time had slipped by.

Dean wasn't there, which was typical. He put us through all of this for nothing. I knew he didn't give a shit about the kids. He never had. The lump in my throat only disappeared when I was in the car driving away. The flood of tears was finally able to escape. The dam I had built up around my emotions had burst.

After a couple of days I had resigned myself to the fact that the kids would be gone for so long. There was nothing I could do about it, so I might as well get on with things and enjoy the break. I discussed my options with my parents but hadn't yet decided on what to do when the children were returned to me after the two weeks with their father.

The next day my decision was made for me.

It was Saturday. My parents were out doing the grocery shopping and I was doing a crossword puzzle at the kitchen table when the phone rang. I answered it. It was Dean.

'You've got two hours to get your arse down here and get these kids,' he boomed into the phone. I had to pull the receiver away from my ear, he was so loud.

'What's wrong? What's happened? Put your mother on.' I didn't know what was going on and was getting flustered. 'Put Kate on.'

'Hello,' Kate said timidly.

'Katie, honey, it's Mummy. Are you all right?' I asked, trying to keep the panic from my voice.

The only answer I received was in the form of barely audible noises.

'Katie?' I tried again – nothing but jumbled confused sounds. I knew something was wrong. She usually talked your ear off on the phone, she was always such a chatterbox.

'Katie, I'm coming to get you, okay?'

I heard the phone change hands at the other end and Dean's voice took over.

'You've got two hours.' He hung up without another word.

I grabbed the car keys and raced out the door, slamming it behind me. I thought of nothing as I made my way down the mountain towards Hampton. All I wanted was to get there as fast as I could. I sped all the way, praying I would not run into any police cars, which would have resulted in a police chase because I wasn't stopping for anyone. It was bad enough having to stop at red lights, and when I was stuck behind a slow driver I understood the meaning of the term 'road rage'. I could have rammed these people off the road quite easily, no trouble at all.

When I arrived and walked through the gate I saw the kids' bags on the porch. Kate and Jack came running from the side of the house. They ran to me and I picked them both up at the same time, walking awkwardly to the car and strapping them in their seats. I then went back for the bags. There was no sign of anyone. It seemed Kate and Jack had been left outside to wait for me on their own. Normally, Sharon would not have allowed that to happen. All I wanted to do was grab my kids and get the hell out of there.

When I returned to Mum and Dad's with Kate and Jack they were surprised until I explained what had happened while they had been out. I had decided my next move on the way back. I didn't care how many laws I had to break or how many orders I had to breach any more. My children could not be put through this again, and neither could I.

I was going to change my name and head back down to Victoria, to a different town though, of course. With my mother's help I dyed my hair from its naturally light strawberry brown to blonde. I also had it cut shorter. I chose a family name and was now Amy Deakin, which was my paternal grandmother's maiden name.

Chapter 11

Two years later Kate, Jack and myself were living comfortably in the Victorian coastal town of Bracken. Kate had started primary school and Jack attended a day care centre while I worked in the local supermarket. We were renting a little three-bedroom weatherboard home close to the beach. I had always wanted to live by the ocean; I loved to swim in the surf. The only problem was that it was freezing cold most of the time, apart from only a few days a year, which made swimming almost impossible unless you had a wetsuit like the surfers. Still, we made good use of the beach and took long walks along the sand and explored in amongst the rocks when the tide was low. Jack wanted to keep everything he found. He hated leaving the starfish behind. I explained to him that they were living things and that they would miss their mums and be sad. He understood when he was told but always forgot when the next thing popped into view.

Kate loved school. She loved to learn and the teachers loved her. They had nothing but praise for her. I ended up having to tell the school everything because Kate had confided in one of her teachers about the 'bad man'. The teachers were quite horrified by our situation. They assured me that Kate would be well taken care of and that if there was anything they could do, I only had to ask.

They were very nice but I failed to see how they could help other than make Kate feel special, which they did well. It was a good start to her education.

Kate and Jack were now also known as Deakin, although I couldn't change their names legally without Dean's permission. I knew hell would freeze over before that was ever going to happen.

I loved working again and had made quite a few friends in the small seaside town. I started smoking pot heavily once more – most of the people I had met did; here there was never a shortage. It came in by the boatload before being unloaded and distributed throughout the state.

I had become very close with one of the girls from work; she was the same age as I was. Cindy and I hung out together quite a bit after work. She would come to my house and when the children were asleep we would have a few drinks and a smoke. We would end up pretty well plastered by the end of the night. We'd put music on and dance around in my sparsely furnished living room like idiots. I was having fun again.

At first Cindy would 'score' for me, because I didn't know any dealers but, after a few months she introduced me to the guy she got the gear from. Cam lived in a run-down shack on a small parcel of land down a long gravel driveway. He was a short skinny guy with blond hair and bucked teeth. Not at all what I had pictured when Cindy had told me he belonged to a biker gang. Later I learnt that Cam was the stepbrother of the top guy. They were close and looked after each other well. If Cam ever ran into any trouble then his brother would sick his cronies onto them: problem solved.

It wasn't the kind of scene I really wanted to be involved with again, but I figured it could come in handy down the track if the need arose. And I needed somewhere to score.

Cam was always playing the guitar. Every time I walked up to his door he could be heard playing a familiar tune. He had three or four instruments sitting on stands in his living room, acoustic and electric guitars with amplifiers sitting by the wall. Sometimes there were other guys playing as well. I would hang around and listen for a while. They were pretty good.

'Do you play, Amy?' Cam asked me one day.

'I had some lessons for a while when I was about ten but that's it,' I answered.

'Wanna learn?' he casually asked.

'Are you offering to teach me?'

'Yeah, if you wanna learn.'

So each week Cam gave me a guitar lesson. It was

heaps of fun once my fingers had adjusted. I remembered the blisters from when I was a kid. That was probably why I had given up so early. The pain of ballet was enough. These guitar lessons with Cam were fun. He was a complete hoot; I was in hysterics most of the time. After eighteen months of lessons I was getting pretty good.

When I went over there and other guys were playing – usually guys from the biker gang – Cam would get me to sit down and jam with them. It got to be a regular event to drink shots of vodka, smoke pot and play music.

This was how I spent my days off work; I only worked a couple of days a week but kept Jack in day care for five days for the break. Over time Cam had extracted bits of information from me regarding my past troubles. He really felt for me, I could see it in his face.

'Do you want me to get someone to fix him up?' Cam asked, seemingly eager at the prospect. I felt excited at the thought, but refused. To see Dean dead or really messed up would be cause for a celebration, but I couldn't be a part of that. I couldn't bring myself to say yes. I wished I could, deep down I wished I could. This is what I had wished, phase three, but I couldn't do it.

On my birthday I went to Cam's to get myself a smoke to celebrate. I handed some money to him and he wouldn't take it.

'No way. It's your birthday. Wait here, I've got something else for you.' He turned and walked away.

I was putting the $50 note into my jeans pocket when Cam came back carrying something that looked suspiciously like a guitar box.

'This is for you.' He placed the large box on the table in front of me and took off the lid.

Inside was a shiny red acoustic/electric Monterey guitar. It was beautiful.

'I can't accept that,' I blurted out, not believing that someone I really didn't know very well could buy me such an expensive present. He sold me drugs and taught me to play guitar – he shouldn't have bought me one.

'Yes, you can and you will. I can't believe that you have been through as much shit as you have,' he paused. 'I can't believe that anyone could treat you so badly. I just wanted to show you that not all people are bad. Not everyone is after anything from you other than who you are.'

Tears began to form in my eyes as he spoke. Nobody had been so nice to me for such a long time. Nobody had said such nice things to me for such a long time. I wanted to hug him, but I didn't.

He lifted the beautiful instrument from the box and handed it to me.

'Play something,' he said.

And I played the first song Cam had taught me: 'Stairway to Heaven'.

I furnished my house by the sea the same way as I had at the farm, purchasing cheap second-hand things wherever I could. I went to quite a few garage sales and picked up many bargains. I scoured second-hand stores for cheap things I could use. After a while I ended up with everything we needed.

I bought Kate and Jack bikes for Christmas with the extra money I had saved from working. I still loved working at the supermarket. I loved the social aspect and was becoming a whiz on the checkout.

During the Christmas holidays, Kate and Jack were looked after by the sister of a woman I worked with. Her name was Shelley and she had two young children of her own. She was married to a shearer who had hurt his back and was unable to work, so they needed the money. Kate and Jack loved going there the days I worked – they did finger painting and they baked cakes and biscuits. Shelley was wonderful with them.

The new school year came around all too soon and it was time for the kids to say goodbye to Shelley and her children and go back to a normal routine. We promised to come back and visit, but we never did.

Two days after school started I dropped Kate off and then took Jack to day care. I went home to get changed into my work uniform and have a coffee before my shift started. The supermarket was only a five-minute drive from home so I left ten minutes before I was due to be there.

As I turned onto the road that would take me through

the main street of town to the supermarket, I noticed an old white Ford with yellow New South Wales number-plates drive past me heading in the opposite direction. It did a quick U-turn and overtook a car to get behind me. I drove slowly through the main street, wanting to see who was in the Ford. I didn't know if I was being paranoid but I had learnt not to take that chance.

Looking over my shoulder had become a natural instinct. I now looked for and noticed things most people didn't think twice about. I slowed down as much as I dared and looked in the rear-vision mirror.

My heart stopped when I saw Dean behind the wheel. There were two others in the car, one in the front passenger side and one in the back seat. I didn't recognise them.

I drove to the end of the street, slowly, as I had been doing. I didn't want Dean to know I had seen him. I turned left and picked up speed; Dean followed. Halfway down the street I stopped the car, got out and ran. I didn't even close the door. I ran into a building with a small police sign attached above the door. Dean wasn't far behind me. I could feel him.

I ran in and started banging my hands on the front desk; there didn't seem to be anybody there.

'Help,' I yelled. 'Help me, please.' I kept yelling until two police officers emerged from a door to my right.

'Help me. He's coming.' I was on the verge of hysteria.

'You fuckin' bitch.' Dean appeared in the doorway. 'I'm going to fuckin' kill you.'

He started coming towards us, anger spreading across his face. Red-hot rage was visible in his eyes. One of the uniformed men grabbed my arm and shoved me through an open doorway. I heard the door lock into place. I could hear shouting for a while but I couldn't tell what they were saying. Their voices were muffled through the heavy walls.

Then everything was quiet. The shouting had stopped. The heavy door swung open and one of the police officers entered the room where I was seated at the table. He came to sit opposite me and asked me to tell him what had happened. He asked me what school Kate was in and which day care centre Jack attended.

'I am going to send a car to pick them up and bring them here. Dean has been told to come back in a couple of hours. We are calling in the magistrate to open the court. We are going to get you an intervention order.'

Great, another one. What did I need with another worthless piece of paper? They didn't work.

The small courthouse was opened and more police were called in. I guessed they might have looked into Dean's criminal record. I had never seen such a reaction to his presence before.

A circle of police walked me the short distance from the police station to the small sandstone courthouse. Dean was already seated at the front of the room and his mates sat behind him.

An elderly grey-haired magistrate occupied the bench.

I was seated at the front of the room on the opposite side from Dean, still surrounded by uniforms. Kate and Jack were back at the station with a policewoman to watch over them.

Kate had not appreciated being picked up from school by a policeman. She was scared and embarrassed. She was angry with me for allowing it to happen, and she'd let me have it as soon as she had seen me. Jack, on the other hand, had thought it was pretty cool, driving around in a police car. They had even put the siren on for him which had resulted in Kate's already embarrassed state increasing.

I had never seen Dean lose his temper in court. Maybe the suit had helped him in other ways apart from making him look handsome and wholesome. He was wearing torn jeans and a black T-shirt today. He had had no time to prepare.

'Are you fucking deaf?' Dean kept yelling at the magistrate, who tried to calm him down by telling him he would be placed in the cells if he couldn't be quiet.

'If I wanted her dead then I would have killed her by now. She's got my kids,' Dean kept yelling.

I was granted an interim order thanks to Dean's behaviour and the case was adjourned for a month to enable both of us to seek legal representation.

After the case, the police escorted me home and told me to pack as many clothes as I could.

'Why?' I asked.

'It's not safe for you to stay here. You need to leave. We can't make him leave but we can protect you,' one of the policemen explained.

Protect me, I wondered, or protect them? They drove us right out of town, hours away, to Glassridge. I was told not to set foot in Bracken again until the next court date.

I was set up in a cabin in a caravan park, one night's rent graciously paid for me by the Victorian police service. They had driven me out of town and paid only one night's accommodation. I was furious.

It was a nice cabin with all the modern conveniences. I wasn't sure, though, how I was supposed to afford to pay for it over the next month, and the police obviously hadn't thought about it. They obviously hadn't thought about my job or the house I was renting in Bracken either.

It was like I was just meant to cease to exist in that town. They had erased me and I had done nothing to deserve it. I was being driven out of town and Dean was getting away with everything, as usual. It was like he had some kind of sixth sense and he knew when I was starting to get comfortable. As soon as a smile appeared across my lips and stayed for too long he swooped to shatter my world. The world I had worked hard to build.

I put Kate and Jack to sleep in the bunk beds that were in one of the two bedrooms in the small cabin. It was clean and cosy. The other bedroom had a double bed, there was a small living area with a couch and television, a small modern kitchen and the bathroom had a flushing toilet and a shower. I couldn't wait to have a shower but the water was scalding hot one second then freezing cold the next. The effort put me in a worse mood than I was already in. I sat on the couch and got more and more pissed off about the events of the day, the more I thought about them. I couldn't help it. My life had been turned upside down and I didn't know what I was going to do. I sat up for most of the night thinking over my dilemma. I couldn't see many options.

I never did go back to the house by the sea. The only time I returned to Bracken was for the court date a month later. I don't know what happened to all our belongings, including the majority of the kids' toys and new bikes. I thought the real estate agent must have sold everything, or given it away. What else could they do?

It was just another thing that needed to be cut from my memory. It hurt too much to think of it. Even though it was only material possessions I was leaving behind, it still hurt. They were mine, but they could be replaced, in time. I had always managed to replace everything – well, mostly everything – in varying degrees of quality but always replaced. I had had to start over three times already. It was heartbreaking. I knew I just had to keep going, I couldn't let it all overwhelm me or I would drown.

The kids and I hung out in the small cabin and got to know Glassridge during the four weeks we had to wait. It was a nice place, a lot bigger than Bracken and had everything Bracken did not. There were shops of all descriptions – Glassridge even had a McDonald's. This pleased the kids no end as it had been ages since they had had Macca's.

Dean didn't turn up to the scheduled hearing for the intervention order so it went ahead without him. It was a different magistrate this time, a younger version. The previous overseer of this case had left some notes regarding Dean's behaviour during the last appearance.

The younger magistrate granted a ten-year restraining order. Kate and Jack had also been included on it. I was surprised because I had always been told that the maximum time a restraining order would be granted for was twelve months. Twenty-four in extreme cases.

Dean wasn't allowed near us, on paper anyway, until 2009. It gave little relief or peace of mind, but it was the first hint of justice – however slight – that I had witnessed since this all began. I knew, though, that I couldn't rely on a restraining order for protection.

I sat in the cabin late that night wondering what to do next; I couldn't stay here any longer. It was time to move on. I looked on the map and decided that I wanted to see more of the southeast.

I couldn't take long finding somewhere to settle now that Kate had started school and she had already missed a month.

The kids had cried for weeks about their toys, bikes and friends. They wanted their own beds and they wanted their videos. It was hard watching them go through losing everything again. It was hard making promises I knew that I might not be able to keep, but I made them anyway. It was probably not the smartest thing to do but I just wanted to ease their pain, even if only for a little while.

I finally stopped in another small town and found a three-bedroom timber house I could easily afford. Pebble Bay was where we set up our new home.

Chapter 12

Pebble Bay is a small coastal town that swells to its limits during the summer season.

Kate was enrolled in the local school and quickly made friends. Jack and I spent our days walking along the beach, exploring the local area.

Once again I scoured the garage sales and second-hand shops to enable me to furnish yet another house. I never had to look far to find a good bargain. Within a couple of months we had most of the essentials, like beds to sleep in. Until we had these, we made do on the floor.

When Jack started school I got a waitressing job during the day at a local café. Reeds was a trendy café that served modern Australian and Asian cuisine. There was always dance music playing too loudly in the background but it was a very popular little place; brightly painted and with a great atmosphere. People went there just to hang out, drink coffee and eat cake. It was a happening place. The place to be seen in Pebble Bay.

I hadn't really become friendly with anyone since I had arrived in town; it was a very cliquey place. If you hadn't grown up there you were considered a tourist, and although it was the holiday-makers who contributed to their livelihood, the locals did not look upon tourists kindly.

It was a lovely and strange town. I didn't want to go and look for somewhere else. I didn't want to move again or uproot the kids so I decided to stick it out and see what happened.

Things improved once I began to work in Reeds. It provided me with the social outlet I craved. There were ten employees at the café and I got along with most of them. Some worked during the day and some at night. The chef worked all the time. The café was open six days a week.

I still played the guitar Cam had given me, though I had never seen him again. Sometimes I wondered seriously whether I should have accepted his offer of wiping Dean off the face of the planet. But there was no use in trying to go back and think of how things might have been if I had made different choices.

When Kate and Jack weren't home and I wasn't working, I took long walks. I would walk to the beach and, depending on the weather, have a swim. I had bought the kids bodyboards but I found I used them more than they did. On hot days I would take a board and drive to the beach. I loved riding the waves. It was exhilarating and I felt free, sliding right onto the sand amongst the foamy water.

I still kept in constant contact with my parents and occasionally with my sisters, who both now had families of their own. I had missed out on it all. If I ever rang Mum and Dad's when everyone was there enjoying a noisy family gathering I felt alone and usually cried afterwards. Christmas and birthdays were the worst. If it weren't for the kids they would have been dark days indeed. I missed my family and hadn't seen them for years. I didn't feel safe going back there and I didn't know if I ever would.

When certain songs came on the radio I fought back tears and some things on the television were a trigger and left me a quivering mess. I knew the triggers; I knew what to stay away from. I tried hard to control my mixed-up emotions. If I didn't I would turn into a complete basket case. I had visions of being carted away in a white van with padded walls wearing a straitjacket, which, incidentally, would have driven me crazier.

I had been working in the busy café for a little over six months when a customer asked me out on a date. Scott was a six-foot-tall, good looking barman at the local pub, and he came into the café almost every day for lunch. Scott had moved to Pebble Bay as an adult, and he had been married until twelve months before. His ex-wife still lived in the town. I hadn't been out in years so I accepted his invitation.

I went to the local supermarket and looked on the large noticeboard, which usually had names and numbers of hopefully responsible teenage girls looking for babysitting jobs to earn some extra cash. I met a couple of them and settled on seventeen-year-old Rhianon. She seemed to be a very nice girl and the kids liked her.

I was so nervous and had no idea what I was going to wear. I stressed out about it all day. It took me hours to choose, taking everything out of my closet; every piece of clothing I owned was strewn over the floor and the bed. All this just to go out for dinner, I wasn't sure the effort was really going to be worth it. I thought about calling the whole thing off but was glad that I didn't.

Rhianon arrived twenty minutes before Scott was due to pick me up. She had brought a couple of children's videos and some junk food with her. Kate and Jack were ecstatic and couldn't wait for me to leave so they could have fun.

I settled on wearing a pair of jeans, a sleeveless white turtleneck and a pair of black boots. I left my hair out which was still a fake blonde colour and had grown a little past my shoulders. I put a bit of make-up on and was not satisfied in the least with what I saw. I rarely was. I hated myself. I hated my body. I hated my face. I hated my scars. How was I ever going to let any man get that close to me again? The thought really scared me. Hopefully I wouldn't have to worry about it; I was having trouble believing that

Scott had seriously asked me out in the first place. Maybe he had been dared to.

I went over a few things with Rhianon, who told me that I had no need to worry about a thing, that she looked after her younger brothers and sisters all the time. She had told me that before, of course, but I was so nervous I had forgotten all about it; I had forgotten everything. I think I was sweating. There was a knock on the door – three loud raps – and my heart skipped a beat. That was how Dean always knocked.

'Are you going to answer that?' Rhianon was looking at me strangely.

I quickly snapped myself out of my trance and went to the door. The knock came again. I took a deep breath and reached for the handle. Behind the door stood Scott, looking handsome in blue jeans and a simple white shirt. I had only ever seen him in his barman's uniform and I must say this outfit was certainly a lot sexier.

In my boots I was the same height as Scott. He had sandy-coloured hair and ocean-blue eyes. His body was muscular and well shaped: his regular morning surf kept him toned and tanned.

'Wow,' he said as I stood aside to let him in.

'What?' I asked, a little too defensively. I was worried enough about the way I looked and now I thought I must have had snot hanging from my nose or something.

'You look great.'

I knew he was just saying that. What else was he going

to say? I thanked him anyway and returned the compliment. He really did look great. I introduced him to Kate, Jack and Rhianon and gave the kids a kiss goodbye, reminding them once again to behave themselves. I told Rhianon that I wouldn't be home too late.

Scott took me to a beautiful Thai restaurant in Knox, which was about a half-hour drive away.

'It's the only one I trust here. You have to go to Melbourne for a really good meal. They have no idea about food in Knox.'

On the way, I heard Scott's personal evaluation of practically every establishment in the small city. He really was passionate about his food.

We ate green curries and drank wine. We laughed a lot and I was grateful that he did not ask too many questions. Apart from where I grew up and bits and pieces from my childhood he knew nothing else. He did ask about Kate and Jack's father, although I quickly dodged the question by saying, 'Oh there is no father. They were an Immaculate Conception.'

He laughed and didn't enquire any further.

After our meal we walked along the esplanade, past the boats moored in the bay. It was a clear night, the dark sky was filled with sparkling stars and there was a light breeze coming off the water. It was calm and peaceful. We weren't the only ones enjoying the lovely night: there were other couples, slowly walking, hand in hand, lovers on moonlit strolls.

We were back at my house at 10.30 and I paid Rhiannon – she had her own car so didn't need a lift home.

'The kids were angels,' she had responded to my question. 'Not one problem. I'm happy to look after them anytime.'

They always were angels for other people. When Rhianon left I went to check on them, both tucked up in their cosy beds. I kissed them gently on their heads as I did every night when they slept.

Scott waited in the living room. When I came back I made the coffee I had promised. We chatted some more and when we had finished our coffees I thanked Scott for dinner.

'I had a really nice time.' I was hoping he would get the hint and leave. He must have read my mind because he got up from the couch.

'Yeah. It was a good night. We'll have to do it again.' He thanked me for the coffee as I walked him to the door.

'So I'll see you soon,' I said, opening the door, feeling as awkward as I had at the beginning of the night.

Scott turned to me and pulled me into his muscular arms. He kissed me tenderly for a long time before releasing me and walking off without a word.

As well as seeing each other when he came into the café, Scott and I continued to go out once a week. Sometimes he took me into Footscray, a suburb of Melbourne, and we went to some fantastic little Vietnamese restaurants.

They looked very authentic and also dirty – it worried me the first time, but they served the most unbelievably tasty food.

I enjoyed Scott's company very much. The first time he stayed the night I made him leave the light off. As I got to know him I was able to tell him about a few of the things Dean had done to me. There were a lot of things I couldn't tell him – or tell anyone – but I had told him about the burns and that I didn't want him to see them. He assured me that he didn't care but I was positive that one look and he would run out the door, never to be seen again.

We made love clumsily in the dark. Scott was slow and careful. He was so gentle it was as though he thought I might break.

Within only a couple of months the kids and I had moved into his house. It was a nice open-plan house. It had a big living area and a kitchen with vaulted timber ceilings. There were two bedrooms downstairs, with a huge bathroom, and upstairs there was another bathroom and an open loft-style main bedroom which looked over the living area. The house was across the road from the beach and at night I loved falling asleep to the sound of waves crashing on the shore.

Scott seemed to get along with Kate and Jack well enough. It was good for Jack, who needed a male role model. Not too long before he had thought his male appendage would fall off because Kate and I did not have one. I had to show him books on biology with pictures and it was only when he started school that he believed me that boys stand up to go to the toilet. It is hard raising any child on your own, but bringing up a boy is tough, especially if there isn't a man around at all. I didn't know what I was going to do when he got older; I had heard stories about the things that happen to boys through puberty. I didn't know if they were true or not and I didn't have any brothers so I knew absolutely nothing about raising a male. My father was really no help at all with this sort of stuff. It embarrassed him.

To start with, the relationship between Scott and I was great, but only a few months later things began to turn sour. Kate and Jack became a real problem for Scott. They cost too much, they were noisy and they woke up too early. It didn't help that the bedroom didn't have a wall. When Scott had a day off and wanted to sleep in, the kids were expected to stay in their rooms and not make a sound until he decided to get up, which was usually any time between ten and eleven in the morning.

They couldn't have breakfast and I couldn't even make a cup of tea. There was no chance of having a shower. It caused a lot of arguments and I felt like the meat in the sandwich. When Scott was around and I was doing something with the kids he would get the shits. He would mope around the house and not speak to anyone. Whenever I spoke to him he would come back with, 'Oh, so you're speaking to me are you?', like a spoilt child.

It was like he was jealous of them. He didn't like them to monopolise my time. He was the youngest child in his family and had obviously grown up having lots of attention and being pampered to death. Actually, his mother still treated him like a child and she didn't like me very much. Apparently nobody had ever been good enough for her Scott. No-one ever quite measured up, least of all this woman with children.

At the time I tried to ignore the bad stuff, just as I had done with Dean. I tried to alter my own behaviour to fit into Scott's image. Nothing worked and I seriously thought there was something wrong with me. A terrible thought struck me one day. Maybe I had an incredible talent for bringing out the worst in people.

It wasn't an altogether unhappy relationship. There were just verbal arguments – it was never physical – usually over Kate or Jack, sometimes both. Even then it wasn't as if Scott was mean to them. He spent quite a bit of time with them doing different things. He took them to the beach and the park. He kicked the football in the yard with them and we had a lot of barbecue dinners together. We also spent weekends at Phillip Island and went to the Formula One Grand Prix in Melbourne. So it wasn't all bad.

Working so close to each other became probably the most difficult thing. If an argument carried over, Scott just couldn't forget about it and he would come into the café and let everyone else know.

I am not saying that I was any kind of saint, because I am far from it. Sometimes I picked fights with Scott just to get back at him, and I started badmouthing him to others. I thought it would be better if I got in first. It was an immature and vindictive relationship.

He started to compare me to his ex-wife. 'Belinda used to do this. Belinda used to do that. Belinda put sliced banana in the salad. Can't you do it like that?'

'NO I CAN'T.' Did he want me to be her? Why wasn't I good enough? Why couldn't I be accepted for who I was? Me, Amy – not Belinda and not the red Toyota who liked to do things I didn't. What was wrong with me?

I think Belinda lived by the philosophy, 'I don't want him but nobody else can have him.' She had started making phone calls to me not long after I moved in with Scott.

For the first few weeks Belinda rang only when Scott wasn't home. She then started ringing to speak to Scott, always for some stupid reason. Did he have the vase her mother had given them? It was probably sitting in front of her holding a thorny rose. Her previous phone calls to me had consisted of her telling me that I was not wanted in town. She had actually told me to go back to whichever two-headed town me and my bratty children came from. I hadn't heard anything so catty since high school.

Belinda was well known in town, well known and popular. Tall, with long blonde hair, she had a tattoo of a rose on her shoulderblade, which she liked to show off by wearing skimpy clothing. For some reason Belinda was the sweetheart, the darling of Pebble Bay. If others didn't think this they certainly gave a good impression of it, and Belinda thought she was too important to be forgotten. Belinda could do no wrong. Belinda was perfect. And if Belinda didn't like you, Belinda was the ultimate bitch.

She started to make my life in the town very difficult. Mothers at the school no longer spoke to me at the gate. When I said hello, they ignored me. Kate and Jack started losing friends; kids no longer asked them over to play and refused to come when invited to our house. Soon after, the locals refused to be served by me at the café, even regulars who I had been serving daily for the past twelve months. Needless to say, I didn't have my job for much longer. Belinda's boyfriend Andrew started getting in on her act, going to the pub and picking fights with Scott.

It was beginning to be a bit like us versus Pebble Bay. Pebble Bay against us. It placed a lot of stress on our already rocky relationship.

One night my car was broken into, the glove box emptied and its contents strewn across the front seat. The only thing missing was the ten-year restraining order against Dean.

'Why would any one want that?' I asked Scott. 'What use is it to anyone?'

'Belinda.' Scott replied without hesitation.

'What would she want with it?' I was confused.

'It's got his address on it, hasn't it?'

Oh my God, he was right. I felt cold. The piece of court-sealed paper had Dean's mother's address on it. If anyone contacted Sharon she was bound to pass a message on to Dean. She wasn't interested in seeing or hearing from the kids without Dean's knowledge. I had always thought about her on birthdays. I knew she loved the kids. I had sent her a letter not long after the ill-fated access visit telling her that if she liked, whenever I got to Sydney we could meet somewhere and I could also send her photos of Kate and Jack. I had got Mum to send the letter from a post office in New South Wales and used the same post office as the return address.

Sharon had written back and Mum passed the letter on to me. In it, Sharon said she couldn't do that behind Dean's back. She would have to let him know. She wrote that she had burnt the letter I sent her because if Dean saw it he would be very angry.

If she wanted to protect her low-life son then so be it. She had ruled herself out of the picture – until now.

'Oh shit,' I whispered. 'She wouldn't, would she?'

'Yeah, she would. I'd put money on it,' was Scott's helpful reply.

Instead of offering support, he was making me feel worse. All my hard work, all the running and hiding and this bitch was going to undo it all. There had been so many times over the past few years, especially when the kids were small, when I would be walking down the street and I'd see someone who looked like Dean from behind. I would grab Kate and Jack, turn and run. I was so paranoid it was pathetic, jumping at every sound, not sleeping for days and then only sleeping when I could no longer keep my eyes open. I hadn't felt that blinding fear for a while now and I didn't want to go back to it, either.

I couldn't move. I was outside with Scott standing by the car, it was morning, Scott was speaking to me.

'Amy, hey, Aim,' Scott was waving his hand in front of my face. I blinked and his blurred features came back into view.

'Come on, let's go inside.'

He helped me walk slowly through the gate and up onto the timber verandah. I felt sick. I quickly pulled myself from Scott's helpful hold and ran through the front door to the bathroom where I released the contents of my stomach.

I vomited every day for the next two weeks. If I didn't already know it was the stress from thinking Dean would be on his way, I would have sworn I was pregnant. Thank God I had taken excellent precautionary measures in that department that lasted five years. I had had an IUD inserted. It was very effective and easy, no thinking about the daily, inconvenient pill.

To make matters much worse I had been trying to give up smoking cigarettes. I couldn't do it alone and had tried the patches designed to prevent cravings, but they didn't work, I still smoked. A new tablet had been released and was supposed to be very good. It had only just become available when I went to the doctor for them.

I hadn't had a cigarette for three weeks. In that time my car had been broken into and Dean probably knew where I was. I didn't need the stress.

With Kate and Jack in bed one night, I sat down to watch some telly and wait for Scott to come home from work. At about nine o'clock the phone rang and I answered it, thinking it would be Scott. He sometimes called when he was leaving work.

I picked up the phone and said hello.

'I know where you are,' a muffled male voice spoke. 'I'm coming to get you.' There was a loud click at the other end as the line disconnected. I stood with the phone to my ear listening to the regular intermittent beeps before there was silence. I still had the phone in my hand when Scott came home two hours later.

The next day Scott was working a double shift and when he left for work he told me that he was going to ring and check up on me so I had to answer the phone. I was worried all day that when the phone rang it would be the same muffled voice on the other end. After sending the kids to school I sat on the couch all day, biting my nails. The door was locked. I didn't move until Scott came home for his afternoon break.

Scott helped me take my mind off everything and when the kids came home from school we had one of his famous gourmet barbecues so I wouldn't have to cook later. He had brought me home a bottle of wine and I drank a couple of glasses with the scrumptious char-grilled chilli chicken burgers he had prepared.

When Scott went back to work I helped the kids get cleaned up and ready for bed. We played a game of Twister and read a book before I tucked them tightly beneath their sheets.

'Meet you in my dreams. Don't let the bedbugs bite. See you in the morning,' we said to each other in unison after kisses and hugs.

'I love you guys,' I called out, leaving the hall light on and closing the door that divided the small hallway from the living room.

I picked up a book and sat down to read but found it hard to focus. I had only read about ten pages when the familiar ringing of the telephone started.

'Hello,' I answered.

'Are you ready to die? It's going to be a bang. Front-page news,' and then the voice disappeared, the connection abruptly cut. I didn't know if it was Dean or not. I just couldn't tell, it was so muffled. It sounded like him, but then again I couldn't be sure.

I put the phone down. I hadn't even lifted my hand from the receiver when it rang again, I picked it up slowly and held it to my ear, I didn't say anything.

'Amy, are you there?' It was Scott. 'Amy,' he had panic in his voice. He kept calling my name, begging me to say something. I could hear the background noise of the pub: clinking glasses and rowdy voices.

'I'm here,' I forced myself to answer him.

'Are you all right? Why didn't you answer me? Did he call again?' His questions shot at me, his voice a little more relaxed now because I had said something.

'Yes,' I said hoarsely, answering all the questions in one, although I wasn't sure how 'all right' I was.

'I'll be there in half an hour, okay?'

I didn't say anything.

'Amy. Will you answer me?'

'Okay, all right.' I forced the words out of my constricting throat.

When Scott hung up I did the same and walked slowly, as if drugged. I was in a daze, floating, not feeling my feet, my mind numb. I moved through the living room to the stairs and drifted up the steep staircase, walking past the queen-size bed into the walk-in closet. I went to the far corner where shoeboxes and spare blankets were stacked against the wall. I sank down in the corner behind the hanging clothes and hugged my knees tightly, resting my chin on them. I stared out the door that led to the bedroom. I couldn't see the familiar contents of the room past the open door. All I could see was darkness. A black hole, a dark space of nothing. I stared into the terrifying space. I couldn't cry, only stare blindly, mind-numbingly, into the dense dark cloud of hell.

I didn't hear Scott come home. I didn't hear him call

out my name, in search of me. I didn't hear him find me curled up in the closet. I didn't feel his hands touch me. Or his strength as he lifted me from the floor and placed me on the soft bed. I was still curled up, now lying on my side in the foetal position.

I didn't feel his lips kiss my cheek or his fingers stroke my hair. The only thought that persisted in my diminishing mind was, 'I can't do this any more. I can't, I just can't.'

My mind had become as dark and as vacant as the space I now occupied. The terrible dark space that Scott had lifted me into and I could not stop him. I couldn't tell him not to bring me in here, I couldn't tell him to leave me alone. I couldn't scream.

In the morning Scott was still sitting beside me, stroking my hair. I heard Kate and Jack downstairs dressing themselves for school. I wanted to move, I wanted to get up and go down to them, but I couldn't. My body would not follow my instructions.

'I'll get the kids to school. You stay there.' Scott sounded very tired. Had he really sat with me all night? I don't know what he was thinking when he told me to stay there: I couldn't move, I was paralysed. I was going nowhere.

Scott made the kids their breakfast and drove them to school. When he came back he called in sick at work and bundled me up in the car, driving me to the hospital.

Hours later I was diagnosed as suffering from a nervous breakdown and was sent home with a prescription for antidepressants.

After a couple of days I was moving around again and Scott went back to work. The medication made my limbs respond to my demands but did little to dispel the dark cloud that hovered above me, waiting to swallow me up.

Because the Easter school holidays would be starting in a week Scott had found a replacement to work for him so he could spend the two weeks at home with me. I was having trouble coping with the kids. I was having trouble coping with everything. I couldn't even make a cup of tea without forgetting how to, halfway through the basic process.

On the first day of the holidays the phone calls started again. Scott had taken Kate and Jack to the shop to get a few things when the first one occurred. There was no voice on the other end of the line this time. No muffled, deep, male voice to torment me, just silence, which in a way was so much worse.

The cloud lowered around me, thicker than ever, choking me, suffocating me. I had stopped taking the anti-depressants a couple of days before. They had begun to make me want to sleep all the time.

The cloud took over, taking control of me. Poisoning my mind, controlling my actions. I got a glass of water, picked up a small box from the kitchen bench, and carried them to the dining table. My movements were slow. Deliberate. My brain unthinking. My body unfeeling. Clouded by darkness, a growing tumour. I picked up some writing paper and a pen and pulled one of the heavy wooden chairs out from under the table. I sat on the padded fabric-covered seat and began to write, the pen seeming to move across the paper without any effort on my part. I wrote two words.

I'm sorry.

Then I began emptying the box. Taking the foil-backed plastic bubble packets and popping the tablets out onto the table. One by one I swallowed each of the 40 tablets designed to cut nicotine cravings.

'I'm sorry,' I said after the last tablet slid down my throat with the last of the water. My gaze shifted to a photo of my children. I got up from the chair and drifted to the bookcase where the photograph in the maroon frame sat. I picked it up and looked into the smiling eyes of my babies. What had I done?

With the frame still in my hand I took a couple of steps toward the front door. My head felt heavy, a huge weight on my sagging shoulders. I clutched the photo to my chest, my arms wrapped around it. I stopped moving. My vision blurred. I took another drunken step before crashing to the floor, just as Dean had done after drinking the laced hot chocolate I had made him. I wasn't unconscious; my eyes were open, but I couldn't move. I was lying on my stomach, one arm still underneath me holding the precious portrait close to my heart. My body was a lead weight unable to respond to anything. My vision was becoming increasingly clouded.

I don't know how long I lay there, sprawled on the floor, before Scott returned. I think I had drifted out of consciousness when I felt a hard slap on my face. I willed my eyes to open.

I had been rolled over onto my back, still holding the photo of Kate and Jack. Scott was supporting my head, a desperate expression etched across his face.

'Oh my God, Amy. What have you done?' Concern filled his voice. He gently placed my head back onto the floor.

'I'll be back in a minute. Hold on Amy, okay? You hold on. Do you hear me?' Scott held my face between his hands. 'Amy, you hold on.'

Scott got up quickly and ran out the door. Luckily Kate and Jack had not come inside. They probably stayed out to play with the many kids who lived in the street. They were rarely in the house on weekends. They would stay outside riding bikes and rollerblades, kicking the footy and chasing dogs.

I heard Scott come back with someone else. I could hear a woman's voice.

'Shit. What's she taken, Scott?' I opened my eyes to see Debbie, the neighbour. Our kids always played together. It was only the people in the street who were nice to me. They had got to know me and didn't listen to the small-town gossip.

'Scott, call an ambulance. *Now.*' Debbie was shouting at him. She was only a tiny little thing. She was only about five feet tall but she had a big voice.

I don't remember anything more until the ambulance arrived and the paramedics roused me from oblivion. There were two men working on me while I lay still on the lounge room floor. Checking vital signs, searching for responses.

Once they were satisfied, they lifted my leaden body and placed me on a trolley, wheeling me to the waiting ambulance. The man who climbed in the back with me said to Scott, 'We'll just cruise in, mate. She's stable, so there's no need to hurry. You can meet us in there.'

The doors were closed and the ambulance began to move. Halfway to the hospital something went wrong. I felt my body started to shake uncontrollably. I heard the man in the back with me start yelling at the driver. His hands were all over me, working quickly. I heard the sirens go on and all I remember after that is playing in a golden garden with tiny angel children, my children.

Chapter 13

I woke up in intensive care. There seemed to be tubes entering every part of my body. Tubes were providing me with fluids, oxygen and charcoal to soak up the drugs in my system. Apparently I had been in emergency for over four hours. The doctors didn't really know how to counteract the new drug. They hadn't seen anybody overdose on it before. My heart had stopped when the seizures hadn't. Scott had been told I might not make it. It would be touch and go. My parents had been called and were on their way.

It had been almost twenty hours since I had been brought in on the verge of death.

I had been told when I had tried to ask that Kate and Jack were with Debbie. It was hard to speak; the tubes prevented it and hurt my throat. The nurse placed a small chip of ice in my mouth to ease the discomfort.

Scott was allowed to come back into the room when

the doctors had finished examining me. They were looking for any permanent damage the drugs might have caused. Everything seemed clear and they were happy. The tube was removed from my throat, as the charcoal was no longer needed. The oxygen tubes and drips remained.

'You're a very lucky young lady,' said one of the doctors. He was wearing small round glasses, like the ones John Lennon wore, and they didn't suit him at all. They looked very strange.

'We'll be sending the Psych Department down to have a bit of a chat with you Amy, okay?' said the other doctor. He seemed to have a much better bedside manner than his colleague, or maybe just more of a tolerance for people who try to take their own lives.

I felt stupid now. I didn't want to die, I really didn't. I felt stupid and uncaring. What kind of a mother was I?

Scott was grateful to see me awake.

'Your parents will be here tonight,' he said to me as he sat on a chair next to the hospital bed. When he wasn't talking, the only sounds evident were those of the machines I was hooked up to.

'Why did you do it, Amy? Why?' Scott had his elbows resting on the edge of the bed, his head in his hands. 'You scared me.'

Mum cried when she saw me and Dad didn't know what to do. He looked uncomfortable, standing by the bed looking down on me, his vulnerable and sad, sad daughter. His eyes mirrored my own, lost, as if he recalled an unhappy memory of his own.

They didn't stay long. I needed some sleep and they wanted to pick up Kate and Jack from Debbie's and take them to their hotel room. I was glad about that, the kids would be happy to see them, and Mum and Dad would be able to at least ease some of the confusion they must have been feeling.

I had not yet seen my children. I didn't want them to see me like this, helpless. I was meant to look after them, to protect them from harm, and I had failed.

Mum and Dad promised to see me early in the morning. Scott was going to watch the kids for the day. The hospital psychiatrist – ironically, his name was Dr Downer – wanted to see the three of us together: Mum, Dad and me.

I had spent a couple of hours with the doctor earlier and after hearing my story he was surprised I hadn't tried to top myself before.

'You have been through more than anybody deserves. You should be proud, Amy,' he had said.

'Proud?' I questioned. How could I be proud of anything, how? I didn't feel proud, I felt as worthless as Dean had said I was, worthless and hopeless.

'You have excellent survival mechanisms. If you didn't,

you wouldn't have survived this long, and you have survived a long time, with two children. You have to realise how much courage you have. Then you will realise you can do anything. It was all bound to catch up with you sooner or later. I am just surprised it took this long, you're an amazing young woman, Amy.'

Dr Downer had a kind smile that made his emerald green eyes light up. His voice was gentle, soothing. I guessed he was about 40. He had dark hair and a caring personality, and was easy to talk to. I didn't feel stupid talking to him; he didn't make me feel stupid. Everyone else was wise in hindsight; everyone else said they'd seen this coming and that I should have, too. It is easy to judge what you would do from the outside. On the outside you have a clear head, on the inside though, there seems no way out of the maze.

Dr Downer explained to the three of us that there was really no easy solution to my problem other than hard work. I needed to feel safe and there were a few other things I could do to protect myself, which he would go through with me at another stage. He said that in his opinion I was and had been for quite a few years suffering from post-traumatic stress disorder. It is a common condition for women living with domestic violence. He likened it to being in a war – apparently war veterans suffer the same symptoms, especially those who have been in direct combat: flashbacks, nightmares, depression, the past controlling the present.

I felt a little better knowing that what I had had a name and I wasn't the only one. This wasn't a lone journey; people had come through it before me, and I wasn't crazy, I just thought I was.

The illness, though, was only the symptom of a greater problem, and I said as much to Dr Downer.

'Amy,' he said. 'Control the symptoms and you control the way you handle the problem. Control the symptoms and you will see other ways of dealing with the problem, you'll start to see other choices, other ways.'

No longer reliant upon machines, I had been taken out of intensive care and placed in a general ward. The emergency doctor with the John Lennon glasses had wanted the Psychiatric Department to admit me to their unit. Dr Downer wouldn't hear of it. I wasn't crazy – I had just been through years of abuse. Being placed in a locked unit with seriously mentally ill patients would only succeed in bringing me down, making me worse. According to Dr Downer I needed encouragement and hope.

A few days later he came to see me to discuss safety options. He suggested I change my name completely and try to get a court order to change Kate and Jack's last names, and said he would write a report to the magistrate in support of this. He also suggested putting high-security alerts on my personal information. I would be able to choose a password that would ensure that only those authorised to do so would have access to my personal details. I didn't know I could do this. No-one had told me before that I could.

He also told me about victims' compensation, a large sum of money available to victims of crime where intense suffering has occurred. I fitted the category; unfortunately, though, the time allowed to claim following a physical assault had lapsed. It didn't matter that it was doing anything to my head, it didn't matter that I had been living with it. What was happening to my mind was a lot worse than any physical pain I had endured. What was happening now was more dangerous, in a lot of ways, than physical abuse. Solicitors should have told me about the compensation, though they never did. So I was entitled to nothing, but that didn't matter. I didn't care about money; I cared about happiness and freedom.

Scott didn't come to see me very often in the two weeks I spent in the hospital. He had left his job so that he could spend time with me and help me for a while. I told him that he shouldn't have done that, but he said that it was fine, he could go back when he was ready, they were only putting on a fill-in barman.

That was the day after I had woken up and I had hardly seen him since.

Kate and Jack started coming to the hospital when I came out of intensive care. I was so happy to see them I pulled them close and didn't want to let them go. My parents brought them in every day after that and took them with them at night. The kids gave me presents that my parents had bought for them to give me.

The day I left the hospital I felt so much better, revitalised, in a way. I was still worried and I didn't know whether that all-too-familiar weight would ever leave me. What I left with was information, which led to renewed hope.

Within only a few weeks I had changed my name: first, middle and last. We would now be the Joneses. Like Smith, it was common, a bit like looking for a needle in a haystack, really. My full name was now Sarah Ann Jones. Common.

I had security passwords put on personal records within certain departments, the ones that had the facilities to do such a thing. I had also secured a court date to apply for orders to change the children's surname without Dean's permission being needed.

Finally everything had been done. We had new names once again, and had become different people.

I was surprised it had been so easy to obtain the court order to change the kids' surname. The report by Dr Downer detailing past events certainly helped, as did the fact that it had been so long since the kids had seen Dean and they really didn't know him – all these facts contributed to the court's decision.

Scott had been moody and grumpy since I had come out of hospital and Mum and Dad had gone home after a long, teary goodbye.

I bought a modem and connected Scott's old computer to the Internet. I had realised that information had empowered me and I wanted more. I learnt all I could about post-traumatic stress disorder and about domestic violence. I was amazed at how often it occurred. The numbers were staggering and continue to climb.

I read stories of other women who had lived a similar hell to my own. I was especially astonished by the information I read about children who witnessed violence. It answered my questions about Kate's vivid memories of the past. They would fade in time, but would forever remain in her subconscious. I made safety plans and gathered folders filled with facts.

The longer I sat at the computer the more pissed off Scott became. He started slamming things around the house.

'Why do you keep dwelling on all this shit? It's just going to screw you up even more, isn't it?'

'Do you think I'm screwed up, Scott?' I asked him.

He didn't reply, he just continued to slam things around. I went back to the computer. I looked up sites all over the world dedicated to the prevention of family abuse. One in three women around the world have suffered some form of abuse, usually by a male perpetrator. In the Middle Ages a man was permitted by law to beat his wife as long as he didn't use a stick broader than his thumb.

I didn't want Scott affecting me negatively, depressing me, so I tried to stay out of his way and didn't speak to him very much. It went on like this for months. It got to the stage when the times we did speak to each other, we snapped. We didn't have fun any more. Scott didn't want to go anywhere with me and when I suggested something he refused, finding any plausible excuse he could muster in such a small amount of time.

He went out by himself quite often and when it all got too much for me I walked along the beach, for miles, the fresh ocean air clearing my mind. Maybe the ocean held the secret to my finding the happiness that I craved so much it hurt, maybe it was whispering the answer in its cool salty breeze.

Debbie had been a big help and continued to help out. She would come over to make sure everything was all right and check that I was doing okay. She was a medical receptionist and she knew all the regular patients, having worked there for years. Some of the regulars had developed the habit of joke-swapping with her and Debbie would bring them over. We'd have coffee and a really good laugh.

Being a small town, news travelled fast and it didn't take long for Belinda to find out about what had happened.

Scott stayed out as much as possible. He had started drinking. Apparently he used to be a big drinker but since I had known him he hadn't drunk very much at all. I drank more than he did. His occasional glass of wine with dinner lately turned into a full bottle. I knew that he now spent a lot of time at the pub and at friends' houses drinking. He started blaming me because he had left his job. Resentment is a terrible thing.

'So why don't you go back, Scott? You said you could,' I shouted back at him when he blamed me the first time.

'Well I can't, can I? I just told you that.'

'And I told you that you didn't have to leave your job, *so don't blame me*,' I shouted really loud, and it felt good. I wasn't going to let anyone blame me any more.

~

Drugs still played a big part in my life. I still got high as much as I could, and when that wasn't available vodka always was. I could sit down to a full bottle and down it like water. When depression crept over me that was how I spent my time. Drunk. Anything to keep me from my life.

~

The weather had been terrible. It had rained heavily over the past couple of days. The sky was dark grey and thick storm clouds hung overhead – it didn't look like stopping for some time.

The kids were at school and I was doing the housework, rain pelting down outside. I answered the phone and Belinda was on the other end.

'So, seen your ex yet? I thought someone should let the poor bloke know where his kids are.'

'You bitch. How dare you mess with things you know nothing about? You don't know who you're dealing with, Belinda.' I spat into the phone, my temper growing. How dare she? Who the hell did she think she was?

'Oh, relax. I didn't do it yet but I will if you don't leave. We just thought we'd play a little game with you.' She was laughing. The fucking bitch was laughing. I don't know whether I had ever been as angry as I was right then, even with Dean I didn't get that angry. This woman was screwing with my life.

'And then I find out you're crazier than I originally thought. Only crazies try to kill themselves. Pity it didn't work.' Belinda was still laughing.

I had never had a problem in this town until the first time Belinda laid eyes on me. Debbie thought Belinda was jealous.

'Jealous of what?' I had asked her.

'Jealous of you,' Debbie had looked at me strangely, her head tilted to one side. 'You really don't see yourself, do you?'

Belinda was still laughing into the phone and she seemed to be enjoying herself immensely. I didn't find any humour in what she had helped contribute to. I slammed the phone down, silencing Belinda's cackling. I grabbed the car keys off the bench, put my runners on and walked outside into the rain.

I was going to show Belinda how bloody crazy I was. I parked at the corner of her street and walked two houses down. I stood in her front yard, dripping wet. I should have been shivering from the cold but I was too angry to feel it.

Belinda lived in a timber house on stilts with a narrow

set of steps leading up to the front door. I got to the blue-painted door and didn't bother knocking; she wouldn't have answered it if she had known it was me anyway. I turned the handle and was surprised that it opened.

I barged straight in, muddy shoes and all, leaving big brown footprints on her light grey carpet. I didn't care.

'Where are you, Belinda, you cowardly bitch. If you've got something to say, come and say it to my face,' I yelled loudly.

Belinda had never spoken to me apart from on the phone. She never said a word to me when we happened to see each other in the street. She always hid behind the safe distance the phone provided for her.

Belinda came out of a doorway and into the hallway I was facing. There was a look of shock written on her face.

'Get out of my house,' she said, her voice shaking.

'Haven't you got anything smart to say?' I replied.

'Get out of my house, you really are mental!' She screamed this time.

I stood my ground, not moving as she came towards me. When she was close enough she slapped my face. I slapped her back, harder. She let out an ear-piercing scream.

'You just assaulted me. Get out!' She yelled as loud as she could. Did she not remember hitting me first?

'You have no idea what you've done, do you? You shouldn't screw with people, Belinda.'

'I haven't done anything to you, so leave me alone.' Was she serious?

'You really are a piece of work, aren't you?' I said to her, disbelief in my angry voice.

Belinda slapped me again and I hit her back so hard this time she was thrown to the floor. I was surprised by my own strength, I didn't know I could do that. She got up, still screaming and threw herself at me. She started pulling my hair and I punched her hard in the gut. She doubled over, still screaming. I don't know how the shrieking sound continued to make its way out of her mouth. I straightened her up and held her against the wall.

'*Will you shut up*,' I yelled at her, but she wouldn't, she just screamed and screamed.

I looked at her and realised how pathetic she really was. She looked like a six-year-old being hassled for her lunch money. She was more helpless than I was. I left her standing there, against the wall, and walked out into the rain leaving more muddy brown smudges on her carpet.

That night the police paid me a visit and I was arrested. It was a good thing Scott was home for the kids but he had no idea what was going on. I hadn't told him what had happened.

I was taken to the police station and charged with unlawful trespass and assault. One half of me knew that what I had done was very wrong but the other half of me couldn't help but laugh at the exquisite irony of the situation. Dean had managed to get away with beating me up for years. I paid a visit to a woman who had succeeded in messing with my life in a big way and I now had a criminal record.

I had to look at the funny side. It was getting to the point where nothing surprised me any more, nothing at all. Life really was a game and if you got past the seriousness of it all then you could see how comical it could be.

I was fighting back and a big part of me was proud of that. I felt the power that violence brought. The same power it gave Dean. I didn't want to become a violent person, but I did understand its attraction. It was a better high than drugs.

This incident made me feel a lot less helpless; I could fight back if I had to.

Chapter 14

The court case for the assault and trespass charges was quick and painless. A restraining order was placed on each of us for a period of twelve months. That was all that happened.

Scott thought it was all very funny – the look on Belinda's face when she heard she would also have restrictions placed on her was priceless. It wasn't at all how she was intending for it to turn out, I was sure. She had invited a few of her friends to court to witness my humiliation. She couldn't have guessed it would be her who was made to look more of a fool than I was.

'Eh, wow, nobody has ever stood up to her before,' Scott laughed on our way out of the crowded Knox courthouse. I never heard from Belinda again after that.

Christmas was drawing near. The kids and I had put up the fake green tree and decorated it with brightly coloured tinsel and hanging ornaments. We made paper chains and lanterns to decorate the house. It had been a few weeks since the incident with Belinda, and Scott had turned back into his shitty self. He hadn't bothered looking for another job. He would have picked one up easily. But instead he blamed me at every opportunity for his downfall.

We got into regular yelling matches that finished with him storming out the door. I don't know why I didn't just end it. I think I was scared to be on my own again. Loneliness terrified me.

Scott was drinking more and more. He didn't seem to know when to stop. He would continue to drink until he passed out. The more he did this the more aggressive he became, like he had a constant hangover. I was drinking a lot too, but vodka didn't give me a hangover, and I never passed out. Scott drank wine and beer. I think it was this mixture that made him so sick. I had always been warned against mixing drinks, and I rarely did.

School was due to finish up for the year in two days' time and Kate and Jack were looking forward to the long break. They were also looking forward to the arrival of Santa Claus; I had received their wish lists in October.

Kate's were always about ten pages long. She wanted

everything from a new book to a horse. Jack's were usually a lot simpler. A bike, a footy or a skateboard and he was happy.

I took Kate and Jack to school on their second-last day for the year. Scott was still asleep when I got home so I sat at the computer typing letters to my family. He woke up a couple of hours later and came down the stairs.

'Don't you ever get off that fuckin' thing?' he asked.

'Don't you ever stop fuckin' drinking?' I asked back.

'That's none of your goddamn business,' he yelled.

'Oh, but what I do is yours?' I was sick of people's double standards.

'Everything's more important to you than I am. After everything I have done for you – and all you do is friggin' shit me. Your kids are more important, your fuckin' ex, that computer.' He was going to town, stomping around yelling at the top of his voice, 'this fuckin' thing is more important, isn't it?'

I heard the sound of my guitar and I turned around. Scott held the guitar, plucking the strings hard, as though he was trying to break them.

'Put it down, Scott.'

'What? Scared I'll break it?' He was pulling the strings out further, one at a time, letting them flick quickly back into place against the wood.

'Please put it down, Scott,' I said again, not thinking he would do much other than snap a few of the steel strings.

Suddenly he lifted it above his head and he smashed its beautiful shiny red body on the floor.

'*No*,' I screamed, practically feeling its pain.

A thing of beauty that someone gave to me to fill my soul with music. Someone who saw more in me than anyone else seemed to see. Someone who had once known me, had taken the time to know me. Cam was no angel, but in so many ways he was one of the sweetest people I had ever known. His expensive gift was now lying on the floor in front of me, smashed into pieces.

I looked at Scott, hatred filling my eyes. I stormed past him, brushing him with my shoulder. He twirled around and grasped my shirt, pulling hard. I fell backwards, hitting the carpeted floor on my backside. I got up quickly and turned to face him.

'How dare you?' I yelled.

'How dare I what? Touch you?' he asked. 'What, like this?' He slapped my face.

I couldn't believe it. The bastard had hit me. We were standing near a bookcase. There was a heavy ceramic vase standing on the top of it at about waist height. I grabbed the vase, which was half-filled with water and near-dead carnations, and swung it at him. I wasn't aiming anywhere in particular. I had seen red, and was sick to death of people touching me, pushing me around.

The bottom of the heavy vessel connected with his cheek. It wasn't a big swing; the vase was heavy. The ceramic container barely touched him, but he fell flat to the floor anyway. His eyes closed.

'Oh yeah, right.' I said, looking at him lying at my feet. 'I've frigging been hit harder than that, you idiot.'

Scott didn't move. I still had the vase in my hand, still containing most of the water and rotting flowers. I knew he was bullshitting, there was no way that it could have knocked him out. I tipped the contents over his face, which made him snap out of it pretty fast. He was up like a shot. He looked at me and pointed his finger at me, close to my face.

'I'm not talking to you.'

He didn't wipe the dirty flower water off himself. There were a couple of soggy black leaves stuck to his forehead. I was glad that he walked out because I wasn't sure how much longer I was going to be able to contain the hysterical laughter that had been building since he stood up and spoke.

After I had laughed so hard my sides ached, I walked around the house throwing Kate's, Jack's and my own belongings into bags and once again packed all I could fit into the car.

I left a note for Scott on the table. All it said was, 'See ya.' Then I drove to the school to pick up the kids.

'Why is there stuff in the car, Mum?' Jack asked.

'Well,' I already knew what I was going to do. 'Don't you want to go and see Oma and Opa?'

'Yay,' they both cheered.

Chapter 15

I called my parents to let them know we were on our way. We travelled all night, arriving the next morning. My parents welcomed us lovingly as always. I was tired and in need of sleep. I thought I could have probably slept for three days. I was glad to be back and this time I wasn't leaving.

Amy Marshall was back as Sarah Ann Jones, a different name, and a different person.

Kate and Jack had a busy day with their grandparents while I slept. Mum woke me up late in the afternoon.

'Amy, wake up. Scott's on the phone, he won't stop ringing. I think you'll have to talk to him.'

Excellent, I was half-asleep and had to listen to Scott, but it wasn't Mum's fault.

'Thanks, Mum,' I said, getting up from the bed and following her out of the room. I went to the kitchen and picked up the phone.

'What do you want?' I didn't think there was any point in a greeting.

'Please don't be like that, Amy. Please come back, I'm sorry, I love you.' He loved me? It was the first time he'd ever said that. A few years ago I would have believed him, but not any more.

'You hit me, Scott. That's not love,' my voice was flat, there was no tone in it at all. I really didn't want to be speaking to him; I wanted to go back to sleep.

'I know. I'm sorry. I didn't mean it. Please believe me, Amy. I don't know what got into me.'

Yeah, yeah, this was sounding a little too familiar. I had heard all of the same things before, from Dean. I wasn't falling for it again.

'I don't give a shit how sorry you are, Scott.'

'Please, Amy, give me another chance.' He was pleading, sniffling into the phone and sounding like he was on the verge of tears.

'No, Scott, I told you that if you ever hit me that I would leave. No chances. What didn't you understand?' I had raised my voice a little, hoping he would get the message.

'So you let your ex hit you for years and I only have to do it once and that's it. Not very fair, is it?' His pleading voice had quickly turned into one of anger.

'Fair?' I couldn't believe he thought he wasn't being treated fairly. 'You want to talk about fairness? None of it is fair, Scott. Being hit at all isn't fair. And let me tell you something, Scott.' I was getting louder now. 'You are worse than he is. You knew. You knew everything he had done and then you went ahead and thought you could do it too. Well, you can't. Nobody can, do you hear me? *Nobody*.'

I was really yelling by the end and Dad came into the room to see if everything was all right. I didn't wait for Scott to say anything in reply. I hung up.

Dad hugged me and I cried. I hadn't told them yet what had happened with Scott. They knew now, though, obviously hearing what I had said. It wouldn't have been difficult to figure it out.

Mum took the kids to the park before dinner and Dad and I had a long talk. A talk like we had never had before in my entire life. I learnt more about my father in those two hours than I had in the 27 years since he and my mother had given me life. He made us both a cup of tea and sat me down at the kitchen table.

'You're stronger than you think you are, Amy,' he began, sitting opposite me. 'You are beautiful and courageous and you don't see it, but you need to see it to stay that way. Your mother and I don't want to have to think about burying you again.'

I opened my mouth to protest. I wasn't ever going to do that again, he had to know that, but he wouldn't let me interrupt. He put his hand up to stop me, and he kept on talking.

'Don't say anything. I need to tell you this. A long time

ago I tried the same thing you did, Amy. I tried to overdose on pills.'

Dad went on to tell me the circumstances surrounding his depression. I knew that he had been married before he had met Mum, but I didn't know how badly it had ended and that he had not coped well. I now knew why his eyes had been so sad, looking at me in the hospital bed with tubes everywhere. It must have been a painful memory for him.

'So, I just wanted you to know that I understand that part. Stay away from anything that keeps you down and learn to stay on top of things.'

'I know, Dad, and I'm sorry. Why can't all men be as nice as you are?'

'It's going to take a special man to love you, Amy. You are intelligent and independent; a lot of men don't like that. But don't ever change to suit a man again. You were raised to think for yourself, you were raised to have ambition and to live your dreams. The sooner you see yourself as we see you, the sooner you will love yourself the way we love you.'

Epilogue

I open my eyes. The sunbeams are still filtering their way through the tree tops. Warming me. Guarding me against unhappy memories. Memories of the past, memories I have been afraid to unleash. I sit up, my feet still dangling over the high edge of the cliff. I look at my watch and decide that I have to leave if I want to be at the school in time to pick up Kate and Jack.

I arrive at the 120-year-old school with its sandstone buildings and leafy views. I have a few minutes to spare so I walk to the gate where other parents wait for their children.

When the bell rings, a sea of green- and yellow-uniformed children explode from the classrooms in a rush to get home.

Kate always waits for Jack and they walk together. She is still very protective of her little brother. Kate has just turned eleven and is turning into a right little lady. She is almost as tall as I am and she is more often than not wearing my clothes. It is very frustrating when you want to wear something and it is scrunched up, dirty, on your daughter's floor. My mother calls it payback.

Jack is now eight and has grown into a cute, mischievous boy. Tall and skinny, he doesn't eat much and I find it difficult to buy pants that fit him. He needs a belt to hold them up if they are to fit him in the legs properly.

They are intelligent, popular and well-adjusted children, which is very surprising considering all they have been through. They are very good at school and achieve fantastic marks; they are well liked by teachers and students alike.

Kate still has nightmares occasionally and has been through quite a bit of counselling to help her deal with her unpleasant memories. She is sensitive but still independent. It upsets her when her friends talk about the fun they have with their dads. Sometimes she comes home and cries.

'Do you want to see your dad, Kate?' I ask her.

'It's not Dean I want, Mum.' She calls him by his first name now. 'I want a dad who's nice. A dad who actually loves me.'

Jack, on the other hand, doesn't seem to care. When Kate gets upset he says to her, 'We've got Mum, you know, Kate. She loves us.'

The past eight years have been a constant battle. A constant fight for freedom. A constant struggle. We travelled a total of 10,783 kilometres. In the beginning it had been a new adventure. I wanted it to be an exciting beginning. A new and better life. A second chance. An escape. An entry into the world, a world where good ruled over evil. A world of opportunity. My dreams were big, my hopes everlasting.

'Remember to take your bags in,' I say today as I get out of the car. I have to remind them every day, or in the morning it is a mad hunt for the missing school bag.

We walk up the rocky path from the driveway to the little brick cottage we rent, Jack still talking at a hundred miles an hour, telling me about his day. It has taken forever to make him speak for himself and to stop Kate from talking for him, and now he doesn't ever give me a moment's peace.

'Eight-year-olds have it really tough, you know, Mum.' He is always coming out with wacky stuff like this – a real comedian.

'Geez you're stupid, Jack.'

'Kate, please don't speak to your brother like that.' Kate thinks everything Jack says is stupid; puberty is starting to rear its ugly head. Deep down, though, I know and Jack knows that she loves him.

I go into the kitchen to make popcorn while the kids decide on a video to watch.

It has been two years since I came back here, to my mountain. I stayed with Mum and Dad for a while before renting this cosy cottage. It has three bedrooms, a small living area and kitchen. All I need.

I am almost 30 and for the first time in my adult life I feel alive. I have found myself, and I like the person I have found. I've had tough times and am a better person for it.

I have learnt that there is always a purpose behind life's experiences. Everything I have been through has made me who I am today. I needed to learn how to die in order to learn how to live.

I don't hate Dean any more – I pity him. And all the devil temptations sailed away with the fear. I no longer need drugs or alcohol as a crutch to live day to day. Instead, my drug is life: that is the best high of all.

I see blue skies in heaven, not the dark familiar clouds of hell.

I have everything I need: my family, the long craved for feelings of happiness.

And popcorn. I pick up the bowl of freshly popped, buttery corn and go to watch *Harry Potter* for the hundredth time with Kate and Jack.

I place the bowl of popcorn on the coffee table and sit between my kids, putting my arms around them.

'I love you guys,' I say.

'I love you too, Mum,' says Kate as she kisses me on the cheek.

Jack hugs me tightly around the middle.

'I love you too, my sweet little Mummy.'

'I am not afraid of tomorrow,
For I have seen yesterday.
And I love today.'

– William Allen White